D1636706

ALSO BY GUY DAVENPORT

A Table of Green Fields
(Stories)
Available from New Directions

7 GREEKS

881 S497s

7 Greeks

Penfield Public Library
1985 Baird Rd.
Penfield, NY 14526

rt/oy

7 GREEKS

TRANSLATIONS BY GUY DAVENPORT

Archilochos • Sappho • Alkman

Anakreon • Herakleitos • Diogenes

Herondas

A NEW DIRECTIONS BOOK

Copyright © 1976, 1978, 1979, 1981, 1991, 1995 by Guy Davenport
Copyright © 1980 by The Regents of the University of California

All rights reserved. Except for brief passages quoted in a newspaper, magazine, radio, or television review, no part of this book may be reproduced in any form or by any means, electronic or mechanical, including photocopying and recording, or by any information storage and retrieval system, without permission in writing from the Publisher.

Versions of these translations have appeared before: Archilochos in the magazines *Poetry* and *Arion* and as a book, *Carmina Archilochi* (Berkeley and Los Angeles: University of California Press, 1964); Sappho as a book, *Sappho: Songs and Fragments* (Ann Arbor: University of Michigan Press, 1965); Alkman in *Arion* (Winter 1969). Lukas Foss and Richard Swift have separately set some of the Archilochos fragments to music, and Swift has made a song of Alkman's "The valleys are asleep and the mountaintops."

Anakreon was first published in *Conjunctions: 6* and as a book by the University of Alabama Parallel Editions, 1991. *Herakleitos and Diogenes* and *The Mimes of Herondas* were published by Grey Fox Press, 1979 and 1981 respectively.

Manufactured in the United States of America
New Directions books are printed on acid-free paper.
First published as New Directions Paperbook 799 in 1995.
Published simultaneously in Canada by Penguin Books Canada Limited.

Library of Congress Cataloging-in-Publication Data

7 Greeks / translations by Guy Davenport.
    p.   cm.
  Contents: Archilochos — Sappho — Alkman — Anakreon — Herakleitos — Diogenes — Herondas.
  ISBN 0–8112–1288–2
  1. Greek literature — Translations into English.   I. Davenport, Guy.
PA3621.A13   1995
881'.0108 — dc20   95–4227
                                                                   CIP

New Directions Books are published for James Laughlin
by New Directions Publishing Corporation,
80 Eighth Avenue, New York 10011

FIELD PUBLIC LIBRARY

Contents

Introduction

Of the Greek poets of the seventh century BC we know almost nothing and none of their poems has come down to us entire. Archilochos was a professional soldier from the Aegean island of Paros; Sappho a member of a distinguished family on Lesbos, an island off the coast of Asia Minor; and Alkman was a slave and choirmaster in the Lydian city Sardis before he emigrated, or was sold to, Sparta, where he wrote the two hymns, to Artemis and Hera, which assure him a place all his own in literature.

Archilochos is the second poet of the West. Before him the archpoet Homer had written the two poems of Europe; never again would one imagination find the power to move two epics to completion and perfection. The clear minds of these archaic, island-dwelling Greeks survive in a few details only, fragment by fragment, a temple, a statue of Apollo with a poem engraved down the thighs, generous vases with designs abstract and geometric.

They decorated their houses and ships like Florentines and Japanese; they wrote poems like Englishmen of the court of Henry, Elizabeth, and James. They dressed like Samurai; all was bronze, terra cotta, painted marble, dyed wool, and banquets. Of the Arcadian Greece of Winckelmann and Walter Pater they were as ignorant as we of the ebony cities of Yoruba and Benin. The scholar poets of the Renaissance, Ambrogio Poliziano and Christopher Marlowe, whose vision of antiquity we have inherited, would have rejected as indecorous this seventh-century world half oriental, half Viking. Archilochos was both poet and mercenary. As a poet he was both satirist and lyricist. Iambic verse is his invention. He wrote the first beast fable known to us. He wrote marching songs, love lyrics of frail tenderness, elegies. But most of all he was what Meleager calls him, "a thistle with graceful leaves." There is a tradition that wasps hover around his grave. To the ancients, both Greek and Roman, he was The Satirist.

We have what grammarians quote to illustrate a point of dialect or interesting use of the subjunctive; we have brief quotations by admiring critics; and we have papyrus fragments, scrap paper from the

1

households of Alexandria, with which third-class mummies were wrapped and stuffed. All else is lost. Horace and Catullus, like all cultivated readers, had Archilochos complete in their libraries.

Even in the tattered version we have of Archilochos, some three hundred fragments and about forty paraphrases and indirect quotations in the Budé edition (1958, revised 1968) of Professors Lasserre and Bonnard,* a good half of them beyond conjecture as to context, so ragged the papyrus, or brief ("grape," "curled wool," "short sword") the extraordinary form of his mind is discernible. Not all poets can be so broken and still compel attention.

Like the brutal but gallant *Landsknecht* Urs Graf, both artist and soldier, or the *condottiere*, poet, military engineer, and courtly amorist Sigismondo Malatesta of Rimini, Archilochos kept his "two services" in an unlikely harmony. Ares did not complain that this ash-spear fighter wrote poems, and the Muses have heard everything and did not mind that their horsetail-helmeted servant sometimes spoke with the vocabulary of a paratrooper sergeant, though the high-minded Spartans banned Archilochos's poems for their mockery of uncritical bravery. And the people of his native Paros made it clear, when they honored him with a monument, that they thought him a great poet in spite of his nettle tongue.

Apollo in an ancient conceit read Archilochos with delight and was of the opinion that his poems would last as long as mankind. "Hasten on, Wayfarer," Archilochos's tomb bore for inscription, "lest you stir up the hornets." Leonidas the epigrammatist imagined the Muses hopelessly in love with Archilochos, and Delian Apollo to boot, for how else account for such melody, such verve? Quintilian admired his richness of blood, meaning liveliness, we suppose, and his abundance of muscle. Plutarch in his essay on music places Archilochos among the innovators of metric, and Horace, imitating Archilochos, congratulated himself on bringing Greek numbers into Italy. Pindar called him Archilochos the Scold. Writers as different as Milton, who mentions him in the *Areopagitica* as trying the patience of the defenders of the freedom of speech, and Wyndham Lewis, who spits

---

* Archiloque, *Fragments*, texte établi par François Lasserre, traduit et commenté par André Bonnard, Collection des Universités de France, publié sous le patronage de l'Association Guillaume Budé (Paris, 1958; 2d ed. rev., 1968).

like a cat at his reputation, took his satiric talent for granted without really knowing what he wrote. Hipponax alone among the archaic poets, we are told, has as sharpened a stylus as Archilochos, and Hipponax is remembered for a grim little couplet:

> Woman is twice a pleasure to man,
> The wedding night and her funeral.

Though he is said to have written with venom and, according to Gaitylikos, splashed Helicon with gore, we have no evidence of anything so caustic. We have to take antiquity's word for it, or assume that the Panhellenes were far touchier than we about satire. Certainly their sense of honor was of an iron strictness. To mock, a Greek proverb goes, is to thumb through Archilochos. "The longer your letters, the better," Aristophanes complimented a friend, "like the poems of Archilochos."

It is precisely the tone of Archilochos that gives us a problem with no solution. In 1974 a new poem of Archilochos's was published in R. Merkelbach's and M. L. West's *Zeitschrift für Papyrologie und Epigraphik*. It was discovered on a papyrus mummy wrapping, identified and edited (ten years' work it was) by Anton Fackelmann, translated here as Fragment 18. Its tone would be aesthetically difficult even if we were surer of its meaning. Our fortune in having it at all is immense and vies in importance with the utterly new dimension of lyric poetry which it gives to our tentative and sketchy knowledge of the dawn of European literature. Is it a comic poem, a raucous anecdote with a hilarious punch line? Is it frankly an erotic poem (Peter Green has waggishly titled it "The Last Tango in Paros").* There is nothing in Greek literature like its last three stanzas. We can understand the robust bawdy of Aristophanes and Herondas, the vivid eroticism of Sappho and Anakreon, but these lines of Archilochos — sung in barracks, on the march, in village squares, at singing contests? — are they satire or salacity, private or public? I would like to believe that it is a satiric collision of a love song and a biological fact, the kind of comedy you get if Juliet on her balcony had dislodged a flowerpot in her ecstasy and beaned Romeo below.

Of the man himself we know that he was born on Paros in the

Times Literary Supplement, 14 March 1975, p. 272.

Cyclades in the first half of the seventh century BC. Pausanias knew a tradition that makes him the descendant of one Tellis, or Telesikles, who was distinguished enough to have figured in Polygnotos's frescoes at Delphi, where he was shown with Kleoboia, who introduced the Eleusinian mysteries into Thasos, an island that owes much to Archilochos's family. A Byzantine encyclopedia credits his father with founding a town on Thasos, "an island crowned with forests and lying in the sea like the backbone of an ass," as Archilochos describes it in a poem.

As his name means First Sergeant (leader of a company of ash-spearmen or hoplites), he may have given it to himself, or used it as a *nom de guerre et de plume.* Some scholars say that he was a bastard, accepted by his father, but the son of a slave woman named Enipo. The poems reveal a man who took pride in his hard profession of mercenary, who cultivated a studied lyric eroticism, and had a tender eye for landscape. His companion was one Glaukos, Gray Eyes, and several fragments address him in a brotherly manner. At one time he contracted marriage with a daughter of Lykambes, Neobulé, probably a settlement that would have retired him from campaigning. "O to touch Neobulé's hand!" is the oldest surviving fragment of a love lyric in Greek.

But Lykambes took back his word and the wedding was canceled. All Greece soon knew, and later Rome, Archilochos's bitter poem in which he wished that Lykambes might freeze, starve, and be frightened to death simultaneously. And all schoolboys, before Greek was expelled from classrooms, knew Lykambes to be synonymous with a broken word of honor.

Archilochos was killed by a man named Crow. The death was either in battle or a fight; nevertheless, Apollo in grief and anger excommunicated Crow from all the temples; so spoke the entranced oracle at Delphi.

Sappho's "I loved you once, Atthis, and long ago," Swift's "Only a woman's hair," are sharp in brevity. The rest of Sappho's poem is papyrus dust. Swift could write no more. Fragments, when they are but motes (the unfinished works of a Spenser or Michelangelo are a different matter), touch us as the baby glove of a pharaoh which moved William Carlos Williams to tears, or the lock of Lucrezia

Borgia's hair which drew Byron back day after day to gaze (and to steal one strand for Landor); they "brave time" with a mite's grip, missing by a rotten piece of linen or a grammarian's inadvertent immortality the empty fame of the sirens' song. To exist in fragments and in Greek is a doubly perilous claim on the attention of our time.

The art that we are seeing for the first time in Archilochos has been a skill of the Western imagination for 2,600 years and shows no sign of fatigue or obsolescence. We can see the cut of Greek satire in Cummings, Brecht, Mandelshtam, Jonathan Williams, Myles na gCopaleen. For vigor of continuity it is a tradition without a rival.

Sappho's art, however, is much rarer: it belongs to cultural spring-times and renaissances. Something of its sweetness can be seen in Hilda Doolittle's conscious imitation:

> delicate the weave,
> fair the thread:
>
> clear the colours,
> apple-leaf green,
> ox-heart blood-red:
>
> rare the texture,
> woven from wild ram,
> sea-bred horned sheep:
>
> the stallion and his mare,
> unbridled, with arrow-pattern,
> are worked on
> the blue cloth

Sappho spoke with Euclidean terseness and authority of the encounters of the loving heart, the infatuated eye's engagement with flowing hair, suave bodies, moonlight on flowers. "Mere air, these words," she is made to say on a fifth-century kylix, "but delicious to hear." Her imagery is as stark and patterned as the vase painting of her time: long-legged horses with dressed manes, marching men, ships, women in procession to a god's altar. Her words are simple and piercing in their sincerity, her lines melodically keen, a music for girls' voices and dancing. Never has poetry been this clear and bright. "Beautiful Sappho," said Socrates.

Somewhere, in the white ruins of Sardis or even on an unexamined shelf or a jar still intact in a midden, there is perhaps a copy of Sappho's poems complete. Around the mummy of an Alexandrian landlord or Antinoopolitan pastry cook there are, we can guess, for we have found them there before, shrouds of papyrus that were once pages of books on which are written Sappho's smiling conversations with Aphrodite, songs for girls to sing at the moon's altar, and clear evocations of the most graceful young women in ancient literature, their laughter, their bright clothes, their prayers, their girlish loves for men "who looked like gods," for each other, and for older women, their marriages into Lydian families or with the boy down the street—"tall as Ares," as the gracious epithalamies describe him. In Chaucer's girls of the Daisy Cult,

> As she is of alle floures flour,
> Fulfilled of al vertu and honour,
> And evere like faire, and fressh of hewe;
> And I love it, and ever ylike newe,
> And evere shal, til that myn herte dye,

in Francis Jammes's connoisseurship of *jeunes filles en fleur*, in Whistler's and Henry James's white-frocked American girls, we can taste something of Sappho's charm and of her vision of adolescent beauty. But Sappho's sure hand at finding the peculiarly feminine flounce that sets her wide-eyed "love of all delicate things" within a sensibility all to itself is so rare that perhaps Gertrude Stein alone among the moderns has got anywhere near it, as in "A Sonatina Followed by Another":

I caught sight of a splendid Misses. She had handerchiefs and kisses. She had eyes and yellow shoes she had everything to choose and she chose me. In passing through France she wore a Chinese hat and so did I. In looking at the sun she read a map and so did I. . . . In loving the blue sea she had a pain. And so did I. In loving me she of necessity thought first. And so did I. How prettily we swim. Not in water. Not on land. But in love. How often do we need trees and hills. Not often. And how often do we need mountains. Not very often.

Even this is protected by a deliberate jauntiness, for all its power to convey. Sappho was infinitely freer, and her gods, a passionate family of high inventiveness, urged her on.

It has been many centuries since the last-known copy of her poems was worn to shreds by human hands. By the tenth century of our era one could read in an encyclopedia: "Sappho, a harp player from Mytilene in Lesbos. . . . Some write that she was also a lyric poet."

An older world that, ironically, we know more about than Sappho's, was gone by the time she was born: golden Mycenae, Crete with its labyrinth and bull-leapers, Pylos, and all the kingdoms of Homer's epics. That civilization had drifted away from the west, away from a trouble we do not yet understand (the explosion of Santorini perhaps, waves of Dorian invaders perhaps) but which did not touch Attica or the Ionian islands, where the high spirit of the old culture lived on for a while beyond its burned citadels.

The Cretan love of flowers, cunning craftsmanship, and rich needlework, and the Mycenaean splendor of chariots, soldiery, gold, and ships are part of Sappho's heritage. Athens, when she wrote, was a country town with old-fashioned cyclopean battlements. Sparta, not yet rigid with discipline nor fanatically tough and frugal, was what Athens was to become, a city of music and poetry, of games in which boys and girls alike played naked, for modesty's sake. Greek education began there, and thus our own. But Sappho's island, for all the awakening of a new world, dreamed on in antiquity, in touch with the rest of Hellas yet facing the rich and gaudy Lydian empire on the mainland nearby. From here came Sappho's seven-stringed lyre, and the sweetly melancholy mixolydian mode that by one account she introduced into Greek music, and her friend the tall Anaktoria.

The seventh century is becoming visible to us. It interests us as the age of Pericles and Plato engaged the Victorians, as Rome of the Republic held the gaze of the eighteenth century. The seventh century's perilous interchange of chaos for order, order for chaos, reminds us of our own. Much was dying, much was being born. Isaiah and Jeremiah, moving in a world much larger than Sappho's, roared at the confusion with fire and vision that we understand all too well. The strenuous flexibility of the rhythms of the next three centuries was beginning. Statues were unfreezing from their Egyptiac stiffness; drawing became graceful, calligraphic, paced like the geometric patterns of weaving and ceramics. Iron was pulling out ahead of bronze. Whole armies, not just the captains, could wield swords.

Even deep in the oak forests of Europe where the kings rode on reindeer and lived in houses on stilts with dogs half wolf at their feet, drawing—as the rocks of the Camonica Valley show—was returning in the seventh century to a grace and formality it had not had for a thousand years. This order of the century as it informed its art has become congenial to us through our learning to see Giotto and Altamira, Lascaux and Bulawayo. Within this aesthetic we can place the psychological nakedness of Sappho and her articulation in sunlit space of emotions that we relegate to velleity and aporia.

Spirit, for Sappho, shines from matter; one embraces the two together, inseparable. The world is to be loved. It attracts, we pursue and possess. Its structure contains the goddess Aphrodite, who inspires love, and her children Eros and Peitho, who tend to their appointed duties, the lighting of the fire of love in the heart and the seduction of the beloved. These bright framings of animal lust, of loyalty and mutual trust in the breeding season, have taken more dread forms in the history of man. Here the animal is wholly tamed, resplendent in a civilized gentleness.

The ancient Greeks recognized the ambiguous allegiances of adolescence and accommodated them in tensely idealistic and erotic affairs all the more poignant for being brief. Barracks life and athletic training had long before created in the military caste tight friendships among men like Sappho's among women. Maximus of Tyre saw in Sappho's comitatus the beginning of the cohering spirit that Socrates refined into philosophical clarity. "They both appear to me to have practised the same sort of friendship, he of males, she of females, both declaring that they loved many, for they were captivated by all who were beautiful. What Alcibiades, Charmides, and Phaedrus were to him, Gyrinnó, Atthis, and Anaktoria were to her."

These loves were in all probability an affair of the aristocracy; they did not interfere with marriage. They seem to have sprung up among comrades closely engaged in common activity, the army, schools or, as with Sappho, a cultivated society of high sensitivity. The Greeks were in fact inventing sensibilities that Europe would, in time, transpose wholly to courtship, as when Arnaut Daniel, Sordello, Bertran de Born, and Dante seemed to rediscover romantic love and to incarnate its radiance in a second age of lyric poetry as brilliant, and as far removed from biological process, as Sappho's. *Amabit sapiens*, Lucius Apuleius says in his *Apologia*; *cupient caeteri*. The educated love; others breed. Apuleius is one of the last authors to understand clearly the old love of adult and adolescent, soldier and recruit, teacher and pupil. "It is not lust but the beauty of innocence that captures lovers," though Sappho knew nothing of the Platonism that colors Apuleius. In fact Sappho puzzled him a little: her archaic robustness had already begun to look gauche and a bit outrageous. "Her graceful voluptuousness," says this Hellenized Roman, "makes up for the strangeness of her songs." The world could no longer appreciate the impact of a walking, smiling girl upon the heart, as if she were the charioteers of Lydia in full armor charging.

Nor was Sappho's ingenuous Aphrodite as wildly sweet to a world whose religions moved in confusion, eclecticism, and despair. Sappho's Aphrodite is Botticellian and her Graces dance again in his "Primavera." The flower was the pattern for her sense of beauty; she delighted in the frilled leaves of dill and celery—lace upon a slender stalk, so that her girls seem crossbred with flowers. "She wreathes the rose with encomia," Philostratos says of Sappho; rose is symbol of girl; girl, of rose, "roses pale as the forearms of Graces, sleeves tucked back at the elbow."

Neither Sappho nor Botticelli separated beauty from the intelligence, of which it is the specious film. Bright eyes, bright mind; balanced walk, balanced nature. The perfect unity of strength and grace in horse, ship, and javelineer underlies her sense of the beautiful, and immediately she demands the enveloping appetence that identifies and completes the beautiful, the untranslatable *imeros*, that yearning that was at once love, sexual longing, adoration, and fascination. Never has a poet been as clear about predilections and attractions. A man should have something of tree, of horse, of a god about him; a woman should have the elegance of the rose and the accomplished Graces. Music, water, air, voices, wine—they must be of a crystal clarity. Where the aesthetic departed from these sharpnesses was in her womanly feeling for the soft and tender: all things colored violet or pink, moonlight, fine cloth, wild flowers, and children.

Her Aphrodite laughs. Sexual frenzy was as respectable a passion to Sappho as rapacious selfishness to an American. Few societies have been as afraid of the body as ours, and in the West none has, within history, been as solicitous as the Greek of its beauty. The Egyptian eye first saw dignity and suave elegance in the body, transferring man's millennia of appreciation of the animal's splendor to his own physique. The Egyptian, though wigged in porcelain, braceleted, ringed, and painted, went all but naked; women's clothes kept to the contours of the flesh. It was for the Greek to see the natural growth of the body in full health as a beautiful thing, abhorring all mutilations, scarrings, tattooings, elongations of skull, circumcisions, subtractions of teeth or fingers. The old Aphrodite was fat and long of breast and behind, and the cow was her rich sign. Sappho's Aphrodite was slender, trim of line.

What remains of Sappho, like all of Greek art, is in ruins. But her troubles do not stop there. "The face of Greece," Nikos Kazantzakis has written, "is a palimpsest bearing twelve successive inscriptions: Contemporary; the period of 1821; the Turkish yoke; the Frankish sway; the Byzantine; the Roman; the Hellenistic epoch; the Classic; the Dorian middle ages; the Mycenaean; the Aegean, and the Stone Age." He might well have added, since it is constantly before our eyes, the Counterfeit. Enter the National Museum in Athens; once you are beyond the great Sounion *kouroi* and the bronze Zeus, or Poseidon, poised to hurl his javelin, you are in a forest of Hellenistic sculpture, Roman copy after Roman copy. Like the Winged Victory of the Louvre, what's before you is not only a copy of a copy, but just as likely part real, part conjectural plaster.

At Knossos, deafened by crickets, you see, surrounded by terebinth, dog rose, and oleander, the ruins of Minos's palace. From here Sappho summoned Aphrodite in a hymn, and here now lovely goddesses stage their epiphanies among wild flowers and doves, on wall after wall, in the most beautiful frescoes to have survived from antiquity. Here are throne rooms, chapels, long stairs, great jars, cypress pillars rising in the most transparent of light. Did not Daedalos build these walls? A few miles away is a city so old it has had ten names and answers now to three (Candia, Megalo Kastro, Iraklion); its streets have known Hercules, El Greco, Dorians, and Nazis. Yet beside Knossos it is young.

One looks. These polychrome frescoes, can they have lasted from a time that was as remote to Homer as Tiglath-pileser to us? There is no warning posted that they are twentieth-century reconstructions, yet they are, like practically all the rest of the surrounding stage set. The charred originals, themselves pieced together by painted plaster to eke out the design, are in Iraklion. Some frescoes are less than a tenth Knossan, as blackened as Sappho's papyrus and parchment fragments, nine tenths the extrapolation of the reconstructor. If they look surprisingly Art Nouveau, that was the style prevalent at the time of their restoration. And these columns, rooms, stairs, balconies? They are so much the work of Sir Arthur Evans, the Stalin of archaeology, that one despairs of knowing Minoan from Victorian Imaginary Minoan.

At Phaistos, across the island, nothing has been counterfeited, and all is as flat as time has worn it. "There will always be some," John Bowman says in his *Guide to Crete*, "who feel that Sir Arthur Evans carried his reconstruction rather too far."

Scholarship until quite recently did the same thing with Sappho's texts. As Sir Arthur's artists found a bull's ear and horn painted on a fragment of wall and then added a whole bull for us to contemplate as an example of Knossan art, so a poem by Sappho can be built up within the ruined places of a text. You can begin by making *Sardis* out of *Sard* (a plausible extension) at the beginning of a fragment, and proceed, conjecturing, emending, guessing. Here, from the workbook in which I began my translation of Sappho, is Fragment 43 done from the reconstructed version of J. M. Edmonds in the Loeb *Lyra Graeca*:

> This white moon in its garden of stars
> Rises over Sardis in the Lydian night
> Where we three in her heart together
> Move in grace,
>
> As in those girlish days when you, her goddess,
> Sang to adoring ears, before adoring eyes.
> Now she walks tall among the wives of Lydia,
> Finest of them all,
>
> As brighter among them in her beauty
> As when an early moon in the first hour of night
> Diminishes with her red hand the brilliant stars
> And finds again
>
> Long fields of flowers, the salt sterile sea;
> And cool dewfall, unfolding the rose, fills the downs
> With parsley and meadows thick with clover bloom.
> There, there she walks,

> In her country, Atthis, among her people,
> And if, holding us in her heart, she calls out in longing
> Across the flower fields, night that has so many ears
> Shall hear her cry.

This is a tempting way to translate. The restorations here are like tuckpointing in a wall still fairly substantial. The art of conjecture can also, as in the following example, rebuild a wall in ruin:

> Heart, be steady till the anthem come,
> For the sovereign Muses would have me sing
> Swift crystal sound to hymn the young
> Adonis slain.
>
> Instead, you stagger in a trance of lust,
> Wild, half human, and by desire disgraced
> Fall down before tongue-tying
> Aphrodita.
>
> Enticement with seducing eyes
> Has poured from her gold two-handled jug
> Honied wine to darken deeper your
> Forgotten mind.

No such poem of Sappho's exists. The papyrus indeed has words that can be read, here and there, and artful conjectures can bridge the gaps between them to achieve a poem like the foregoing. The result, however, is as little Sappho's work as the sentimental ascriptions to her in *The Anthology* which her severest and best editors, Edgar Lobel and Sir Denys Page, omit as spurious.

They also omit the fragment that all the world knows, the one that the parrot in Isak Dinesen's *Out of Africa* recited in Greek in a Chinese brothel, and which Burns seems to answer in his melancholy

> *The wan Moon is setting behind the white wave,*
> *And Time is setting with me, oh.*

—the poem that might be Endymion speaking or a woman who has given up hope that her lover will come, as the paths are now too dark to follow:

> *The moon has set, and the Pleiades.*
> *It is the middle of the night,*
> *Hour follows hour. I lie alone.*

Whoever wrote it (it may be part of a folk song), I follow an old tradition in leaving it among Sappho's poems.

There is so little of Sappho that the reader with beginner's Greek can read the substantial fragments in an afternoon. There are many fine translations of Sappho in English (though none that includes all the fragments), and the only excuse for making a new one lies in the richness of her poetry. Each translator performs not so much a linguistic as a critical act, the closest possible rendering of an appreciation. Many of the fragments are mere words and phrases, but they were once a poem, and, like broken statuary, are strangely articulate in their ruin.

I have generally followed the text as given by Lobel and Page, *Poetarum Lesbiorum Fragmenta* (Oxford, 1963), and additions from Page's *Supplementum Lyricis Graecis* (Oxford, 1974), and am indebted to his *Sappho and Alcaeus* (Oxford, 1959). One can only contemplate with humility the labor that lies behind every printed line of Sappho. I have separated one two-line fragment back into the discrete lines that some editors place together (*I loved you once, Atthis, long ago / You seemed then to me to be an ungainly little girl*), and I have distributed the index of first lines of poems that appears in the Bibliographical Fragment, Lobel-Page 103. Several times I have given alternate translations, under Roman numerals, since no English version of language so remote in idiom and estranged in culture can be in any sense wholly accurate or final.

My starting point was the poems and not the Greek language, my knowledge of which is functional rather than philological. I have followed no strict theory. My intention everywhere has been to suggest the tone of Sappho's words. Had I not accepted as an outer limit to transposing meaning from Greek to English the rule that one must not tamper with grammatical integrity, I could justify, utterly beyond the pale of scholarship, taking the half-visible imagery of Fragment 119, for example, and, using the multiple possibilities for what the torn words might have been in their wholeness, making such a poem as:

> In yellow frock and yellow shawl,
> Stole of topaz and peach-flower hat
> Knit in your hair like a ring of stars,
> In crocus sash and mulberry vest,
> Sandals red as amber wine,

> You stand in the orchard as
> Delicate as the flowering trees.

This is assuredly not Sappho nor an accepted mode of translation, but it is (or might be, if the guesswork has been lucky) an example of her imagery, much as one displays in a museum ornaments of Mycenaean gold without knowing what they are or how they were articulated in their day. The reading of Sappho is surrounded by passionate dispute in which I am unqualified to join; my translation therefore is without any authority except the dubious one of sentiment.

Alkman, born in Sappho's Lydia and a resident in a city where Archilochos would have felt at home, Sparta, is something of a mixture of those two. Like Sappho he wrote songs for girls to sing; like Archilochos he looks at the world with a tempered eye. I have not translated all of his one- and two-word fragments, and I have made multiple translations of his great *Hymn to Artemis of the Strict Observance*, first, to graph the text (found in an Egyptian tomb at Saqqâra in 1855, part of a funerary library presumably to be at hand on Resurrection Day) as literally as possible, indicating lost portions; second in octosyllabic couplets to indicate something of the music and intricate imagery; third, to conjecture the full shape of the poem (the myth it deals with can be found in Pausanias) with no attempt at translating; and fourth to make the sparest possible faithful version, to show how phrase follows phrase.

This amazing hymn was sung at the Feast of the Plow by girls dressed as doves. They would have sung (as we gather from the poem) in rivalry with an opposing choir. All over Greece we find all endeavor taking the form of a contest, an *agon*. Before the age of Archilochos, Sappho, and Alkman, we hear of contests of trumpets, city against city, the splendor of which tantalizes the imagination more than all the kings and archons in the history books.

Alkman's congeniality is in his celebration of the table, the fireside, old-fashioned cooking, and—with a resigned affability—the arthritic good humor of his old age. Goethe admired and imitated his lyric about night coming on and the sleep of animals and birds. Aristotle records that Alkman suffered terribly from lice. My translations were made from Antonio Garzya's *Alcmane: I Frammenti* (Naples, 1954) and in part from Bruno Lavagnini's *Aglaia: Nuova Antologia della Lirica Greca da Callino a Bacchilide* (Turin, 1964).

Anakreon is a poet whose fame and stature come from a collection of poems he did not write. The Anakreon translated here is not the poet who inspired and was imitated so beautifully by Belleau, Ronsard, and Herrick. It was not discovered until the nineteenth century that their "Anacreon" (first printed in Paris in 1554) was an Alexandrian imitation, or homage by a group of poets, that was misunderstood to be a text of Anakreon himself from the Middle Ages forward. This pseudo-Anakreon has been one of the most persistent and rich classical influences of them all. His tradition has been alive — is still very much alive — since the sixteenth century. A history of this influence (as, for instance, Michael Baumann's *Die Anakreonteen in englischen Übersetzungen*, Heidelberg 1974) touches every period of English and American poetry from Puttenham to Thoreau. These sixty poems are now called *The Anacreonta*, and are understood to be an anthology of imitations, never meant to deceive, but to honor.

What we have of the real Anakreon (who lived in Teos, now Sighalik in Turkey, and later in Athens, in the sixth century BC) is precious little, and that is in fragments: six ruins of lyrics on papyrus, 155 brief quotations from other writers, mainly grammarians, and one line, partly conjectural, written on a vase painting. Obviously nothing — neither tone nor imagery nor meaning — is certain in these piecemeal remains of a great poet admired by all antiquity.

Of Herakleitos we know only that he lived in Ephesos between 540 and 480 BC, and that he wrote a book dedicated to Artemis, fragments of which have survived through quotation by later writers. The astuteness and comprehensiveness of his insight into the order of nature have commanded attention for 2500 years, exhibiting a freshness for every generation. Plato counted him among the transcendent intelligences, as did Nietzsche, Gassendi, Niels Bohr, Spengler. His presence as a spirit in both modern poetry (Eliot, Pound, William Carlos Williams, Hopkins) and modern physics makes him peculiarly a twentieth-century guide, one of our daimons.

There are many studies of Herakleitos, and many translations. This one hopes merely to provide the simplest and most transparent English equivalent for the Greek that I can manage.

In Fragment 69 I have departed from literalness and accepted the elegant paraphrase of Novalis, "Character is fate." The Greek says that ethos is man's daimon: The moral climate of a man's cultural complex (strictly, his psychological weather) is what we mean when we say daimon, or guardian angel. As the daimons inspire and guide, character is the cooperation between psyche and daimon. The daimon has foresight, the psyche is blind and timebound. A thousand things happen to us daily which we sidestep or do not even notice. We follow the events which we are characteristically predisposed to cooperate with, designing what happens to us: character is fate.

Among the tombs that line the road into Corinth, Pausanias says in his *Travels*, you can see in a stand of cypress and pine near the city gate the grave of Diogenes of Sinope, the philosopher whom the Athenians called The Dog, "a Sokrates gone mad."

He died at Corinth in his eighty-first year (some say ninetieth), a slave belonging to Xeniades, who bought him from the pirate Skirpalos (or, according to Cicero, Harpalus). "Sell me to that man," Diogenes had said at the slave market, "he needs a master." Diogenes had come up for sale when he was captured at sea, on his way to Aigina. In the world at that time, as now, kidnapping for ransom was a Mediterranean enterprise. Diogenes was a stray, a citizen of no city-state, a man without property or kin.

He seems to have welcomed slavery. He became the teacher of Xeniades' sons, a member of the family. "A benevolent spirit has entered my house," Xeniades said.

Diogenes was born in 404 BC in Sinope on the Black Sea, the modern Sinop in Turkey. His father, an official at the mint, was convicted of debasing the coinage, and the family was disgraced and exiled. Diogenes made his way to Athens, where he took up the jibe of being an outcast's son by saying that he, too, was a debaser of the coinage: meaning that, as a philosopher, his business was to assay custom and convention and sort the counterfeit from the solid currency.

He studied philosophy under Antisthenes, a crusty type who hated students, emphasized self-knowledge, discipline, and restraint, and held forth at a gymnasium named The Silver Hound in the old garden district outside the city. It was open to foreigners and the lower classes, and thus to Diogenes. Wits of the time made a joke of its name, calling its members stray dogs, hence *cynic* (doglike), a label that Diogenes made into literal fact, living with a pack of stray dogs, homeless except for a tub in which he slept. He was the Athenian Thoreau.

All of Diogenes' writings are lost: some dialogues, a Republic, and his letters. What remain are his comments as passed down through folklore to be recorded by various writers. These have obviously been distorted, misascribed, and reworked. The ones I have chosen are from Diogenes Laërtius and Plutarch.

He was a public scold, a pest, a licensed jester. He was also powerfully influential as a moral and critical force. It was at a school of Cynics in Tarsus that a Roman Jew named Shaul Paulus learned to command rhetoric, logic, and rigorous candor. We can even hear the sharp voice of Diogenes in his turns of phrase. Diogenes had said that the love of money was the metropolis of all evil; Paul, that the love of money was the root of all evil.

Diogenes and Alexander the Great died on the same day: a traditional belief that shows a curious affinity. Alexander said, "If I were not Alexander, I would be Diogenes," meaning, one supposes, that if he could not have all of the world, he would have none of it. Neither knew anything of compromise. They were perfect specimens of their kind.

Athens in Diogenes' long life changed from the brilliant epoch of Euripides and Sophokles, to a city in Alexander's empire, soon to be replaced as the intellectual center by Alexandria. Sokrates drank the hemlock when Diogenes was five. Plato, aged 80, died when Diogenes was 57. He was 48 when Alexander was born, 68 when Alexander came to the throne. He invented the word cosmopolitan, to designate himself a citizen of the world.

Though we knew that in ancient Greek culture there was such a thing as a *mimos*, or mime played by a single maskless actor taking all the parts, probably in city squares of an afternoon or on small stages in wine shops, it was not until 1890 that archaeology recovered a

script of any of them—seven scripts, in fact, with titles native to and
characteristic of the long tradition of European comedy from Aris-
tophanes to Samuel Beckett, *The Matchmaker*, *The Whorehouse
Manager*, *The Schoolmaster*, *Women at the Temple*, *The Jealous
Woman*, *A Private Talk Between Friends*, *The Shoemaker*, all miracu-
lously intact in column after column on a papyrus scroll. There are
fragments of six more mimes on the same scroll, but they are too
botched and torn to be made anything of. Another text for one of
them (*The Dream*) was found later at Oxyrhynchos, in almost as bad a
condition as the text on the scroll. The author of these playlets was a
poet named Herondas, or Herodas, about whom we know nothing at
all, neither his city (Kos or Alexandria, perhaps) nor when he lived
(the evidence points to the third century BC). As for his name, its
scant occurrence favors Herodas. I've chosen Herondas as having a
more decisive pronunciation in English.

The papyrus scroll with Herondas' mimes on it was bought in
Egypt by the British Museum's diligent scout E. Wallis Budge, one
of the crack buccaneers of archaeological discovery when the rules of
the game were to bring home the bacon by hook or by crook. Budge
bought the scroll from Coptic tomb robbers, who had filched it from
the grave of some important Egyptian of the early Roman period. It
was customary to await resurrection with one's library to hand. Alk-
man's great odes, for instance, were found in a funerary collection of
this sort, as well as the text of the Egyptian Book of the Dead for
which Wallis Budge is best known.

The scroll is actually the account sheets of one Didymus, a bailiff
in the Roman colonial administration. Its style of handwriting,
thought by Herondas' first editor to be of the first century AD, is now
considered by his most recent editor, I. C. Cunningham, who de-
scribes it as "a small, plain bookhand, with corrections by the first
hand and by at least one other hand," to belong to the second century
AD. On the back of the scroll, in an economic use of good papyrus,
Didymus had copied out a kind of personal anthology of choice texts:
Aristotle's treatise on the Athenian constitution, the odes of Bac-
chylides, some orations of Hyperides, and thirteen mimes by Her-
ondas.

It was the Aristotle that most excited the curators at the British
Museum: a unique text known previously only by quotations from it

by classical writers. Frederick Kenyon, the great papyrologist, transcribed and published all these texts in 1891. The classicist Walter Headlam brought out a scholarly edition of Herondas, with translation, in 1922, and this remained, until Cunningham's edition in 1971, the authoritative text. Because of his richness of diction and vividness of realism, Herondas has been the subject of much scholarship. He has not, however, enjoyed much of a reputation beyond the classicist's lamp. If, as in Cunningham's judgment he is "not an author of outstanding importance or a poet of the first rank," and if, in Frederic Will's assessment he is "the least edifying of the Hellenistic poets," he is nevertheless an abundantly interesting, superbly vigorous poet.

The first step toward seeing him as he must be seen is to imagine a performance. We live in the age of Picasso, who has given us a new vision of the classical world's acrobats, mimes, street actors and singers as they have survived through the unbroken lineage of festival, Italian comedy, the circus. The same figures who cavort at Mardi Gras throughout civilization today could be seen before Aristophanes was born—we have the evidence of painted vases to guide us here—wearing the same carnival costumes, hilarious masks, impersonating the same kind of comic types. We live in the age of Fellini, of Beckett, of Marcel Marceau. The ghost of Herondas cannot find us wholly unfamiliar. Just beyond the strangeness of his surface we can easily locate human nature as we know it all too well.

Were we Alexandrians of the third century BC, citizens of a center of commerce and learning, a polyglot city on the Mediterranean, we would know the public mime as a matter of course. Imagine a broad, level area between buildings, with steps at each end, paved and with a chinaberry tree for shade, where a dog can have a nap, nursemaids can gossip while their charges romp, delivery boys can have a quick game of knucklebones, the kind of congenial little space that still keeps its Greek name, *plateia*, in Mediterranean languages (*place*, *plaza*, *piazza*). Here the mime would set up his business, perhaps with drum, fife, or lyre to collect an audience. He must depend on everybody's imagination to transform the air around him into a school, a room, a law court. He acts without a mask, but certainly with make-up. Some basic props serve him as he changes from character to character—hats, shawls, wigs, a walking stick. Mimicry is his art. The pleasure he gives is that of recognition of type. Once a human being has become fixed in his reactions and is predictable, he has become the matter of comedy.

Herondas is thus working in the tradition of Theophrastos and Menander. He has no political ground, like Aristophanes; no history or ideologies mingle with his art. New Comedy was portable anywhere, and proved to be as native to Rome as Athens, to London and Madrid. It is the art of Jonson and Molière, of Waugh and Wodehouse. Herondas (as he seems to say in *The Dream*) considered himself to be reviving the satiric art of the poet Hipponax, who lived three centuries before him, and who can be bracketed with the master satirist Archilochos. It was the spirit of Hellenism to be retrospective, to restore and polish more vigorous art from previous times. Theokritos his contemporary, whose eclogues can be thought of as mimes (and may have been so performed in aristocratic households and at literary gatherings), and Kallimakhos, also his contemporary, were imitators of what they imagined to be a classical period, a golden age which they were reproducing in silver.

A play comes alive in performance only. Herondas would seem to admit of a wide range of interpretation by an actor. The stage directions which I have made up for this translation assume that these mimes were close to the art of Peter Sellers, of Zero Mostel, and Lily Tomlin—farces deliciously rendered by a master impersonator of types. It may well be, of course, that the acting was more savagely satiric—something close to the acid wit of the Goya of the *Caprichos*, one of which might illustrate *The Matchmaker*. Most of Herondas' interpreters, especially Will and Cunningham, see Herondas as a much darker figure than I do. I see no morbid overtones of sadism in *The Schoolmaster*, only an irate mother with a lout of a son to be disciplined. I can see nothing bawdy in *The Shoemaker*, only women trying on every shoe in a shop without buying any. I see nothing vilely obscene in *The Whorehouse Manager*, only a gloriously absurd plea by a half-literate businessman whose rhetoric is giving the judges a headache.

The very successful skits of the Roman actor Luigi Proietti, called "A Megli Occhi, Please," is probably a fairly close approximation of what Herondas' theatre was in Alexandria in the third century BC. Proietti assumes one part after another. His props are all in a box—

wigs, hats, coats—and his transformation from Calabrian farmer to blowhard politician to American Country Music Singer are made before the audience. Playing without a mask, and without the traditional cloth phallos of the comic actor, Herondas' actor would have approached the realism of our time more closely than any other kind of theatre in antiquity. The recovery of his texts happened in the heyday of British pantomime, of the music halls with their turns and comic skits, of Marie Lloyd, practitioners of his very art. And when he was first published in 1922, the mime was having a renaissance: the silent movies. Now, while the silent mime has masters like Marcel Marceau, and amateur mimes can be seen performing around the Beaubourg in Paris (the old stamping grounds of the Commedia dell' Arte in its day), and mimes are popular with theatrical groups everywhere, it is worthwhile attempting to make the first mimes to have survived from antiquity better known.

Headlam's translation of 1922 is into Edwardian diction and prose; the Knox translation of 1929 (Loeb Classics) is, in Cunningham's laconic judgment, "unhelpful." Louis Laloy's translation into French (Budé) lacks color and verve. I have translated the mimes—the Greek is *mimiamboi*—into decasyllabic lines in rough imitation of Herondas' "limping iambs," trying for phrasing that an actor might say. Herondas' style is either antiqued (presumably to sound like his master Hipponax) or, as I would like to believe, solely on a hunch, in a particular Ionic vernacular, perhaps that of Kos. His words are tightly elided, his phrasing economic, always expressive, idiomatic, and frequently vulgar.

In his version of humanity in all its weakness we can recognize practically everything. It was a world that thought slaves comic in what it supposed to be their shiftlessness, a world that delighted to detect pretension, that charted every minim of movement outside one's social bounds. Battaros the whorehouse manager is comic because he is too stingy to hire a lawyer; it is also clear that he imagines himself to be as eloquent as any lawyer he could have hired. In all the mimes we see the characters as they cannot see themselves, and yet we understand very well how they think of themselves. Bitinna in *The Jealous Woman* sees herself as a generous woman sorely wronged; we see her as an indulgent woman who has spoiled her lover and has only herself to blame if he has an exaggerated notion of his charms. All of

ARCHILOCHOS

1
Sergeant to Enyalios,
The great god War,
I practice double labor.
With poetry, that lover's gift,
I serve the lady Muses.

2
My ash spear is my barley bread,
My ash spear is my Ismarian wine.
I lean on my spear and drink.

3
Let him go ahead.
Ares is a democrat.
There are no privileged people
On a battlefield.

4
This island,
        garlanded with wild woods,
Lies in the sea
        like the backbone of an ass.

5
Listen to me cuss.

6
Pallas Athena and our strong arms,
That victory. From hill to hill in retreat

We walked backward under their javelins
Until we reached the rampart of stones
She, Zeus's daughter, led us toward.
We attacked later, chanting hymns
Of Mytilenian Apollo, while they,
Keeping their courage with harp and song
Fell back to their hill, withered by arrows
We crossed a harvest of our dead.

7   [*A rag of paper,*
         but]

         Bright clean air.
         For you are

         A brave man
         And honorable.

         Wandering
         Aimlessness
         Of evil.

8   What hair styles among
         All this jackass backsided
         Sabazian pederasty.

9   With ankles that fat
         It must be a girl.

10   When the fight's with those hard Euboians,
         No bow-strings' whine or snap of bow-notch
         Or whip of sling do you hear, but a delirium
         Of Ares, sword work and spear sticking,
         The tall Euboians famous for their knives.

11   Like Odysseus under the ram
      You have clung under your lovers
      And under your love of lust,
      Seeing nothing else for this mist,
      Dark of heart, dark of mind.

12   As a dove to a sheaf of wheat,
      So friends to you.

13   His mane the infantry
      Cropped down to stubble.

14   These golden matters
      Of Gyges and his treasuries
      Are no concern of mine.
      Jealousy has no power over me,
      Nor do I envy a god his work,
      And I don't burn to rule.
      Such things have no
      Fascination for my eyes.

15   [*Shredded paper, but*]
      Whittles
                to carry
      [*here teething moths
      have passed*]
            I repulse
      Your great kindness
      [*holes*]
      Kindness.

16   Shield against shield,
      Keep the shield-wall tight.

And the gift of death
They bring, let no man take.

17   She held
                a sprig of myrtle she'd picked
And a rose
That pleased her most
Of those on the bush
And her long hair shaded
                her shoulders and back.

18   [   ]
Back away from that, [she said]
and steady on [   ]

Wayward and wildly pounding heart,
There is a girl who lives among us
Who watches you with foolish eyes,

A slender, lovely, graceful girl,
Just budding into supple line,
And you scare her and make her shy.

O daughter of the highborn Amphimedo,
I replied, of the widely remembered
Amphimedo now in the rich earth dead,

There are, do you know, so many pleasures
For young men to choose from
Among the skills of the delicious goddess

It's green to think the holy one's the only.
When the shadows go black and quiet,
Let us, you and I alone, and the gods,

Sort these matters out. Fear nothing:
I shall be tame, I shall behave
And reach, if I reach, with a civil hand.

I shall climb the wall and come to the gate.
You'll not say no, Sweetheart, to this?
I shall come no farther than the garden grass.

Neobulé I have forgotten, believe me, do.
Any man who wants her may have her.
Aiai! She's past her day, ripening rotten.

The petals of her flower are all brown.
The grace that first she had is shot.
Don't you agree that she looks like a boy?

A woman like that would drive a man crazy.
She should get herself a job as a scarecrow.
I'd as soon hump her as [kiss a goat's butt].

A source of joy I'd be to the neighbors
With such a woman as her for a wife!
How could I ever prefer her to you?

You, O innocent, true heart and bold.
Each of her faces is as sharp as the other,
Which way she's turning you never can guess.

She'd whelp like the proverb's luckless bitch
Were I to foster get upon her, throwing
Them blind, and all on the wrongest day.

I said no more, but took her hand,
Laid her down in a thousand flowers,
And put my soft wool cloak around her.

I slid my arm under her neck
To still the fear in her eyes,
For she was trembling like a fawn,

Touched her hot breasts with light fingers,
Spraddled her neatly and pressed
Against her fine, hard, bared crotch.

I caressed the beauty of all her body
And came in a sudden white spurt
While I was stroking her hair.

19   Poiseidon rider of horses
Has spared the captain
Of our fifty men.

20   Decks awash,
Mast-top dipping,
And all
Balanced on the keen edge
Now of the wind's sword,
Now of the wave's blade.

21   Dazzling radiance.

22   Pass by,
Highborn sir.

23   Attribute all to the gods.
They pick a man up,
Stretched on the black loam,
And set him on his two feet,
Firm, and then again

Shake solid men until
They fall backward
Into the worst of luck,
Wandering hungry,
Wild of mind.

24   The oxherd picks tarantulas from his oxen,
The cocksman keeps his prick dainty and clean:
The nature of man is diverse and surprising,
Each finding his pleasure where the heart wills,
And each can say, I alone among mankind
Have what's best, what's fine and good
From Zeus, God, Father of men and gods.
Yet Eurymas finds fault with everybody.

25   [   ]
Slime and crud
[   ]
Snot

26   [*The left side
Of a poem:*]

Nasty
Which thinks
Woman
Hatefullest
And father
Dear
Not O
Upon

27   Remember us, remember this earth,
           When with hearts against despair
           Our javelins held Thasos from her enemy.

28   Dripping blood.

29   Miserable with desire
           I lie lifeless,
           My bones shot through
           With a godsend of anguish
           As sharp as thorns.

30   She's as timid
           As a partridge.

31   Hear me here,
           Hugging your knees,
           Hephaistos Lord.
           My battle mate,
           My good luck be;
           That famous grace
           Be my grace too.

32   Whoever is alive
           Is pleased by song.

33   Stirred up and raving.

34   You are too old
           For perfume.

35   And the heart
        Is pleased
        By one thing
        After another.

36   He comes, in bed,
        As copiously as
        A Prienian ass
        And is equipped
        Like a stallion.

37   Their duenna in their midst,
        Those girls
                    wore such perfume
        In their hair
                    and on their breasts
        Even old men
        Desired them.
                And, Glaukos my boy,
        Their cunts
        [*but here the papyrus is torn*]
        A parade of girls
        From that shuttered house
        With all its coming
        And going.
        What shoes!
        [*here the papyrus is too tattered to read*]
        Ignorance
        Of the good
        Of things.

38   You bring home
        A bright evil.

39   But iron bends,
           Too, and that poker
           Is limp as a rag
           Most of the time.

40   Friends hurt
           The most.

41   A few citizens
           Hung back,
           But the majority.

42   There are other shields to be had,
           But not under the spear-hail
           Of an artillery attack,
           In the hot work of slaughtering,
           Among the dry racket of the javelins,
           Neither seeing nor hearing.

43   Be bold! That's one way
           Of getting through life.
           So I turn upon her
           And point out that,
           Faced with the wickedness
           Of things, she does not shiver.
           I prefer to have, after all,
           Only what pleases me.
           Are you so deep in misery
           That you think me fallen?
           You say I'm lazy; I'm not,
           Nor any of my kin-people.
           I know how to love those
           Who love me, how to hate.
           My enemies I overwhelm

With abuse. The ant bites!
The oracle said to me:
"Return to the city, reconquer.
It is almost in ruins.
With your spear give it glory.
Reign with absolute power,
The admiration of men.
After this long voyage,
Return to us from Gortyne."
Pasture, fish, nor vulture
Were you, and I, returned,
Seek an honest woman
Ready to be a good wife.
I would hold your hand,
Would be near you, would have run
All the way to your house.
I cannot. The ship went down,
And all my wealth with it.
The salvagers have no hope.
You whom the soldiers beat,
You who are all but dead,
How the gods love you!
And I, alone in the dark,
I was promised the light.

44   Courtyard barricaded by a wall.

45   You led us
           A thousand strong
           At Thasos.

46   Athena daughter of thundering Zeus
           Brings them courage in their battles,
           That weeping people, every man of them a woman.
           Whereupon, the sun of grace upon them,

They build new houses and clean new fields.
They have retreated, as if by habit,
From land after land, without arousing
The least pity in any possible defender.
Now by the will of all the gods on Olympos,
This island.

47   A coat of wool
That seems woven
Of piddock shell
And dyed purple.

48   Golden hair.

49   [*This shred
Of Alexandrian
Paper, torn
Left side, right side,
Top and bottom,
With holes
In the middle,
Reads:*

You[
    ]if[
river[
    ]so[
I then, alone]

50   Watch, Glaukos, Watch!
Heavy and high buckles the sea.
A cloud tall and straight
Has gathered on the Gyrean mountain-tops,
Forewarning of thunder, lightning, wind.

What we don't expect comes fearfully.
War, Glaukos, war.

51   Yes, yes,
As sure as a poppy's
Green.

52   Zeus is the best priest among the gods;
He himself fulfills what he prophesies.

53   Fields fattened
By corpses.

54   The arrogant
Puke pride.

55   Until,
And,
Mountain tops.

56   Field rations,
Legitimacy,
Heart.

57   Hot tears cannot drive misery away,
Nor banquets and dancing make it worse.

58   From Paros
The lovely
We march.

59　　　Phasinos,
　　　　　　　　　dawn shows,
　　　　　And now it is the Thargelia.

60　　　But for what he did
　　　　　To me,
　　　　　He won't get away
　　　　　Unstruck.

61　　　Butt kisser!

62　　　The highly polished minds
　　　　　Of accomplished frauds.

63　　　You've bolted
　　　　　The door.

64　　　　　]you are busy with
　　　　　of Imbros[
　　　　　　　　]repulses[
　　　　　　]well wishing[
　　　　　And I hope[
　　　　　　]making use of
　　　　　　]busy
　　　　　to drive into confusion[
　　　　　　　　]having[

65　　　There is a fable among men:
　　　　　How a fox and an eagle
　　　　　Joined in partnership.
　　　　　[*three decipherable fragments survive:*]
　　　　　She brought her children a horrible meal.

EAGLE: See that high crag there?
                The rough one,
                        the forbidding one?

To get up there you climb
With nimble wings,
Flying from the earth to
The high rock,
Lifting up thus.

O Zeus, Father Zeus,
                yours is heaven's strength,
And you see the works of men,
                both villainous and law-abiding.
To you the uprightness and sinning pride
Of the animals are significant.

66   A sharp helmsman
            And a brave heart
            With a two-master.

67   Thief and the night,
            Thief and the night.

68   I think
            [   ]
            Know then
                    that I am so minded
            [   ]
            To suffer.

69   Foggy island.

70   What breaks me,
                Young friend,
                Is tasteless desire,
                Dead iambics,
                Boring dinners.

71   Greet insolence with outrage.

72   Soul, soul,
                Torn by perplexity,
                On your feet now!
                Throw forward your chest
                To the enemy;
                Keep close in the attack;
                Move back not an inch.
                But never crow in victory,
                Nor mope hangdog in loss.
                Overdo neither sorrow nor joy:
                A measured motion governs man.

73   The old men are idle,
                And should be.
                Simplicity and stubbornness
                Blunder and prate.

74   Little boy.

75   Medlar trees.

76   To make you laugh,
                Charilaos Erasmonides

And best of my friends,
Here's a funny story

77   The son of
          The fig eater.

78   Moral blindness[
          Miserable[
                 ]worthless[
          Jealousy[
             ]O heart[
             ]and not[

79   Some Saian mountaineer
          Struts today with my shield.
          I threw it down by a bush and ran
          When the fighting got hot.
          Life seemed somehow more precious.
          It was a beautiful shield.
          I know where I can buy another
          Exactly like it, just as round.

80   Twice the age of her apprentices,
          That wrinkled old madam Xanthé
          Is still regarded as an expert.

81   Her hair was as simple
          As flax, and I,
          I am heavy with infamy.

82   Desire,
          Future,

Enemy.
Music:
My song
And a flute
Together.

83   Keep a mercenary for a friend,
           Glaukos, to stand by in battle.

84   Touched girl.

85   That old goat
           Patrolled his own corridors.

86   Everything,
           Perikles,
           A man has
           The Fates
           Gave him.

87   Everything
           People have
           Comes from
           Painstaking
           Work.

88   Recompense.

89   Plums.

90   [*Paper*
       Snowflake:]
       Dwells here
          ]hard fate[
       Participate[

91   When Alkibié married,
       She made of her copious hair
       A holy gift to Hera.

92   There is no land like this,
       So longable for, so pretty,
       So enjoyable,
       Here on the banks of the Siris.

93   The heart of mortal man,
       Glaukos, son of Leptines,
       Is what Zeus makes it,
       Day after day,
       And what the world makes it,
       That passes before our eyes.

94   The cave,
       And henceforth I intend to
       Conduct my life with more order
       [*here the papyrus deteriorates*]
           Line, dog, solitude.
       [*the papyrus gets worse*]
       What can I offer in exchange?
       [*and worse*]
       Against the night-prowler
       Mount guard around your house.
       I have seen him in the streets,
       Plotting burglaries.

95

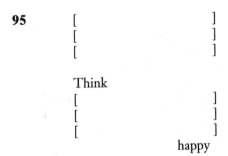

Think

happy

96

To engage with an insatiable girl,
Ramming belly against belly,
Thigh riding against thigh.

97

Zeus gave them
A dry spell.

98

Long the time, hard the work
That went into heaping the wealth
He threw away on whores.

99

Boil in the crotch.

100

Naked.

101

With ships so trim and narrow,
Ropes fast and sails full,
I ask of the gods that
Our comrades have a wind too,
That they meet neither tall wave
Nor reef.
          All fortune be with them.

102   Tenella Kallinike!
                Hail Lord Herakles!
        You and Iolaos, soldiers two,
        Tenella Kallinike!
                Hail Lord Herakles!

103   Wild animals.

104   Our very meeting
        With each other
        Is an omen.

105   Has no liver,
        But, even so,
        Hot as a hornet.

106   [*A thin
        Ribbon of
        Paper*]

        Wine
        [   ]
        Concerns
        [   ]
        Weeps
        [   ]
        Inclines
        [   ]
        Crash

107   Begotten by
        His father's
        Roaring farts.

108   His attachment to the despicable
               Is so affectionate and stubborn,
               Argument can't reach him.

109   Battle trumpet.

110   A man, Aisimides, who listens
               To what people say about him
               Isn't ever going to be quiet of mind.

111   Lying down
               In the olive press.

112   A ditch all around[
                        ]game[
                        ]and speed[
               His inheritance from his father
               That girl tried[
                                ]cooked goose
               Eaten.

113   There's nothing now
               We can't expect to happen!
               Anything at all, you can bet,
               Is ready to jump out at us.
               No need to wonder over it.
               Father Zeus has turned
               Noon to night, blotting out
               The sunshine utterly,
               Putting cold terror
               At the back of the throat.
               Let's believe all we hear.
               Even that dolphins and cows

Change place, porpoises and goats,
Rams booming along in the offing,
Mackerel nibbling in the hill pastures.
I wouldn't be surprised,
I wouldn't be surprised.

114   Venom of a water snake.

115   Gently cock
The trap's spring.

116   Let us sing,
Ahem,
Of Glaukos who wore
The pompadour.

117   Damp crotch.

118   Where, where,
O Erxias,
Is the guidon stuck
Of this company
With its luck shot?

119   Otherwise,
                that stone of Tantalos
Will hang over this island.

120   Not a rampart held.

121   Grief and fasting in anguish
               Strike city street and dinner table.
               We complain, we dream, we blame.
               This sea-cyclone calamity,
               This storm-wave pounding our hearts
               —with hiss and thunder together
               It climbed to knock flat
               With an orchard of foam on top—
               Has mauled us and choked us with hurt.
               What are backbones if not ramrods?
               The gods toughen us, Perikles,
               To stand this pain. Fortune, misfortune;
               Misfortune, fortune. Grit your teeth.
               Not all of us need be women.

122   Night.
               The wind
               Blows landward.
               Branches creak.

123   He made all secure against
               High seas and wind.

124   Justice.

125   [   ] take
               [   ] heart and what
               You have [   ]

126   Thasos,
               Calamitous city.

127   O Hephaistos Lord of Fire,
      How awful to be your suppliant!

128   Put down the uproar.

129   Why should the sea be fat
      With my drowned friends?
      Why oil the knees of the gods?
      Why, why should Hephaistos
      The Fire dance his dance
      On this splendid face
      And feast on these runner's legs
      Poseidon the Water has stilled?
      To the ecstatic fire we give to eat
      This fine body wrapped in white,
      Pleasure once of glad women,
      Companion once of Ares, War.

130   Every man
      Stripped naked.

131   Of holy Demeter
      And of her daughter
      The festival attending.

132   Mountain animal.

133   When the people went off to the Games,
      Batousiades came along too.

134   Great virtue
      In the feet.

135   And close to me.

136   The good-natured need no cutlery
               In their vocabulary.

137   worst,
               [   ]
               Lykambes

138   Elegant frog.

139   A great squire he was,
               And heavy with a stick
               In the sheeplands of Asia.

140   Rigidities melt,
               Masts fall.

141   O forsaken and hungry
               People of the city,
               Hear me speak.

142   And no man thereafter
               With the gods.

143   Hang iambics.
               This is no time
               For poetry.

144
Fortune is like a wife:
Fire in her right hand,
Water in her left.

145
Fast foot.

146
Like the men
Of Thrace or Phrygia
She could get her wine down
At a go,
Without taking a breath,
While the flute
Played a certain little tune,
And like those foreigners
She permitted herself
To be buggered.

147
Upon the roads
Of Ennyra.

148
But, to you, this new thing
[   ]
Weigh in the balance
[   ]
Pleas[ure]

149
Seam of the scrotum.

150
Into the jug
Through a straw.

151   Sparks in wheat.

152   Kerykides his
               [   ]
               Quiv[er]

153   You drink a lot of unmixed wine
               That you haven't paid for,
               And weren't invited to share,
               Treating everybody as your dearest friend,
               Greed having supplanted any shame
               You once had.

154   [*The right-hand
               Line endings
               Of an elegy:*]

               moves against;
               staunching,

               pointed penis
               I, as usual,
               situate;
               suffice.
               the city,
               therefore you imagine
               we establish beauty.

155   Eaten by fleas.

156   She sweetened
               Her voice.

157 He turned.

158 Sabazians
Of the
Elegant
Hair.

159 Of the sons of Selles.

160 Humpbacked
Everytime he can.

161 Deer-heart.

162 He's yoke-broke
But shirks work,
Part bull, part fox,
My sly ox.

163 Idle chatter.

164 This, this
We cannot do.

165 Illusionist in language
And pretentious buffoon.

166 The crow was so ravished by pleasure
That the kingfisher on a rock nearby
Shook its feathers and flew away.

167   The thrones, there,
Of great Zeus,
And his rocks
For throwing.

168   Seven of the enemy
were cut down in that encounter
And a thousand of us,
mark you,
Ran them through.

169   They'll say I was a mercenary,
Like a Carian. Such was life.
Don't call the medics over.
I know a way, not theirs,
To get a swelling like that down.
Listen here, now. No? Forget it.
They'll say I was a mercenary.
Is there clean linen for a shroud?

170   One sizable thing I do know:
How to get back my own
With a man doing me wrong.

171   Ignorant and ill bred
Mock the dead.

172   With what springs
In my legs
I leapt the rocks.

173   Keep a quiet heart.
We move into battle.

Come down among us,
        O Zeus!
The ground is our blood.
Long ships in the bay.

174 Their lives
Held in the arms
Of the waves.

175 Erxias, Defender, how can we muster
Our scattered troops? The campfires
Lift their smoke around the city.
The enemy's sharp arrows grow
Like bristles on our ships. The dead
Parch in the sun. The charges are bolder,
Knifing deep into the Naxos lines.
We scythe them down like tall grass
But they hardly feel our attacks.
The people will believe that we accept
With indifference these locust men
Who stamp our parents' fields to waste.
My heart must speak, for fear
And grief keep my neighbors silent.
Listen, hear me. Help comes from Thasos,
Too long held back by Toronaios;
And from Paros in the fast ships.
The captains are furious, and rage
To attack as soon as the auxiliaries
Are here. Smoke hangs over the city.
Send us men, Erxias. The auguries
Are good. I know you will come.

176 Truth is born
As lightning strikes.

177   Against the wall, fists on hips,
           They leaned in a fish-net of shadow.

178   Sword [
           [   ]
           was placed.

179   Scallop.

180   Wood carved
           To curve.

181   [   ]feet
           [swear!]
           [   ]

182   With Aphrodita
           Audacity wilts.

183   Fox knows many,
           Hedgehog one
           Solid trick.

           Aliter:
           Fox knows
           Eleventythree
           Tricks and still
           Gets caught;
           Hedgehog knows
           One but it
           Always works.

184   In the hospitality of war
We left them their dead
As a gift to remember us by.

185   [   ]
from what
[   ]

186   I hold out my hand
And beg.

187   I weep that the people of Thasos
Are in trouble;
The Magnesians
Are not my concern.

188   Beautiful [
[   ] consider [
  ] and [

189   Teaches the law
Of Crete.

190   And may the dogdays
Blister the lot.

191   Kindly pass the cup down the deck
And keep it coming from the barrel,
Good red wine, and don't stir up the dregs,
And don't think why we shouldn't be,
More than any other, drunk on guard duty.

192   Charon the carpenter,
               Citizen of Thasos.

193   The Cretan.

194   [   ] my [
               Wander [
               [   ] just as [

195   What a burden off my neck!
               What a joy to escape marriage!
               Another time, Lykambes,
                       father-in-law almost.
               I can't bring you to your knees.
               Honor presupposes a sense of shame,
               And that you haven't got.

196   [*A scrap
               Of paper:*]

               Slavery
               Not for me
               But then.

197   Here's a fable, O Kerykides,
               With a cudgel for a moral.
               A monkey was no longer welcome
               In the society of the animals,
               And went away, all alone.
               Whereupon the fox, his mind
               Thick with mischief and plots,
               Began hatching a little scheme
               [   ]
               Water in one hand, fire in the other,

cursing the fate of overseers, servants,
[   ]
The Carpathian, the martyr[
[   ]
Just ahead, there was the trap
[   ]
And a cage of iron [

198   [   ]
         [   ]
         How?
         [   ]
             ] paying

199   Myself the choir-master
         In the chant to Apollo,
         Sung to the flute in Lesbos.

200   Tall Megatimos,
         High Aristophon,
         Pillars of Naxos,
         O Great World,
         You hold upright.

201   Grape.

202   With head thrown back and long throat,
         Crying Euaí! in the Baccanalia.
         [   ] strong heart
         [   ]
         [   ] of curious craft
         Having remained [
         [   ]
                     ] houses [

203   He went away, leaving behind a band of seven
            To get Peisistratos' son home, men who
            Kept order easily with zither and fife.
            He had led them into Thasos to steal back
            The tribute of gold from the raging Thracians:
            Great success, for them, for which the people
            Paid with grief.

204   From dawn onward
            Each drank.
            It was the feast of Bacchus.

205   As one fig tree in a rocky place
            Feeds a lot of crows,
            Easy-going Pasiphilé
            Receives a lot of strangers.

206   They chased him
            Down the mountain.

207   One half,
            One third.

208   Utterly unrefined.

209   A hummock
            Of a bulge
            At the crotch,
            That diner
            On eyeless eels.

210   Mega [
                    ] slavery [
           Ex [

211   There goes
           That cornet player.

212   There's no man she hasn't
           Skinned alive.

213   Now that Leophilos is the governor,
           Leophilos meddles in everybody's business,
           And everybody falls down before Leophilos,
           And all you hear is Leophilos, Leophilos.

214   Tree t[runk]
                    ]and comp[anion
                ]jawbone[

215   Fortune save us from
           These hairy bottomed fellows.

216   Tender horn.

217   How did you become *so* bald,
           Not even a hair on your nape?

218   Fight! I want a fight
           With you as a thirsty man
           Wants water.

219   What a behind,
               O monkey!

220   Imposter.

221   Lykambes' daughter
               To the furthermost village.

222   In copulating
               One discovers
               That.

223   [   ]
               He replied.

224   Season follows season,
               Time grows old.

225   Old and
               At home.

226   It's not your enemies
               But your friends
               You've got to watch.

227   I knocked him out the door
               With a vine-stump cudgel.

228   [Wa]x soft.

229   Servant to the Muses.

230   [   ]wor[k]
            Toward Thasos

231   No man dead
            Feels his fellows' praise.
            We strive instead,
            Alive, for the living's honor,
            And the neglected dead
            Can neither honor
            Nor glory in praise.

232   O that I might but touch
            Neobulé's hand.

233   Nightingale.

234   Curl hung
            In curl.

235   Paros,
                    figs,
                            life of the sea,
            Fare thee well!

236   Soon [   ]
            [   ] dogs

237   The lion ripped him open,
            Poor fellow, as soon as

He entered the cave,
And dined on his tripes.

238   Let us hide the sea-king's gifts,
            The wrecked dead Poseidon brings.

239   Swordsman and murderous son
            of the blood drinker Ares.

240   Arou[nd]
                    ]toward Thasos
            Accomplishment[

241   Biting sword.

242   Courage comes with the man
            Or he's no soldier of mine.

243   Lips covered with foam.

244   How it has all crashed together,
            Panhellenic disaster,
                            here on Thasos!

245   From there.

246   Women eager
            To recline.

247   Jackass hot
            To mate.

248   Rhinoceros.

249   And I know how to lead off
            The sprightly dance
            Of the Lord Dionysos,
                the dithyramb.
            I do it thunderstruck
            With wine.

250   Arthmiades,
            This present take,
            Wine jugs and wine.
            A man of glory,
            Precise with power,
            Wherever among men
            Your might strikes,
            Astonishment grips
            Who sees.

251   Retreat, confusion,
            That army.
            They were strong.
            Hermes saved me.

252   Apollo our protector,
            Slay the wicked.

253   You can't even cross a river
            Without having to pay a toll.

254   Lyk[ambes]

255   Sons scythed down
              By the governor.

256   The child of
              Married people.

257   Soothing.

258   In jeopardy on both horns.

259   No more does this smooth flesh stand slant and bold
              Now that it's withered, and I am old.
              It quickens still at splendid eyes,
              But its seed bag's dry, and it will not rise.
              Cold winds and winter drive us on.

260   Papa Lykambes,
              What's this you've thought up?
              What's distracted the mind
              You once had?
              Mind? You're a laugh.

261   You've gone back on your word
              Given over the salt at table.

262   May he lose his way on the cold sea
              And swim to the heathen Salmydessos,
              May the ungodly Thracians with their hair

Done up in a fright on the top of their heads
Grab him, that he know what it is to be alone
Without friend or family. May he eat slave's bread
And suffer the plague and freeze naked,
Laced about with the nasty trash of the sea.
May his teeth knock the top on the bottom
As he lies on his face, spitting brine,
At the edge of the cold sea, like a dog.
And all this it would be a privilege to watch,
Giving me great satisfaction as it would,
For he took back the word he gave in honor,
Over the salt and table at a friendly meal.

263   And are you willing to be whipped
        Now that you've broken your promise?

264   I consider nothing that's evil.

265   Father Zeus,
        I've had
        No wedding feast.

266   I've worn out
        My pizzle.

267   Desire the limb-loosener,
        O my companion,
        Has beat me down.

268   Voracious, even,
        To the bounds
        Of cannibalism.

269   I overreached
                 And another
                 Bears the bother.

270   What demon tracks you down,
                 What anger behind this terror?

271   Against
                 [   ]
                 In the heart.

272   Strong lords
                 Of Naxos.

273   No more
                 Your face blooms
                 Soft. Lovely,
                 It withers.

274   Overlook my ways.
                 I'm Countrified.

275   She's fat, public,
                 And a whore.

276   Uninspired but sentimental
                 Over one sadness or another
                 As a subject for his poems;
                 The voluble poet whets his stylus.

277   Curled wool.

278   In time of shame,
               Can you spare me the evil?
               Kindness flows both ways.
               Woman, woman,
               Why do you keep me here,
               Why this road, of all,
               And why do you care at all?

279   How many times,
               How many times,
               On the gray sea,
               The sea combed
               By the wind
               Like a wilderness
               Of woman's hair,
               Have we longed,
               Lost in nostalgia,
               For the sweetness
               Of homecoming.

280   So thick the confusion,
               Even the cowards were brave.

281   Birdnests
               In myrtle.

282   I despise to see a tall,
               Swaggering general
               With a beard of curls.

Give me an officer
Who's short and bow legged,
With his feet planted well apart.

283   Give the spear-shy young
Courage.
Make them learn
The battle's won
By the gods.

284   Raise your arms
To Demeter.

285   Now your apronstrings won't tie,
We know your ways.
Hipponax knows them better than any,
And Ariphantos,
Who was spared smelling the thief
Stinking of the goat he'd stolen,
By being away at the wars.

286   Well, my prong's unreliable,
And has just about stood his last.

287   Upbraid me for my songs:
Catch a cricket instead,
And shout at him for chirping.

SAPPHO

1   Aphródita dressed in an embroidery of flowers,
Never to die, the daughter of God,
Untangle from longing and perplexities,
O Lady, my heart.

But come down to me, as you came before,
For if ever I cried, and you heard and came,
Come now, of all times, leaving
Your father's golden house

In that chariot pulled by sparrows reined and bitted,
Swift in their flying, a quick blur aquiver,
Beautiful, high. They drew you across steep air
Down to the black earth;

Fast they came, and you behind them, O
Hilarious heart, your face all laughter,
Asking, What troubles you this time, why again
Do you call me down?

Asking, In your wild heart, who now
Must you have? Who is she that persuasion
Fetch her, enlist her, and put her into bounden love?
Sappho, who does you wrong?

If she balks, I promise, soon she'll chase,
If she's turned from gifts, now she'll give them.
And if she does not love you, she will love,
Helpless, she will love.

Come, then, loose me from cruelties.
Give my tethered heart its full desire.
Fulfill, and, come, lock your shield with mine
Throughout the siege.

2   Come out of Crete
And find me here,
Come to your grove,
Mellow apple trees
And holy altar
Where the sweet smoke
Of libanum is in
Your praise,

Where leaf melody
In the apples
Is a crystal crash,
And the water is cold.
All roses and shadow,
This place, and sleep
Like dusk sifts down
From trembling leaves.

Here horses stand
In flowers and graze.
The wind is glad
And sweet in its moving.
Here, Kypris [   ]
Pour nectar in the golden cups
And mix it deftly with
Our dancing and mortal wine.

3   Nothing can take its place in my mind,
This beauty of girls.

4   I loved you once, Atthis, long ago.

5   Graces O with wrists like the wild rose,
           Chaste and holy daughters, come,
           Come among us, daughters of God.

6   When death has laid you down among his own
           And none remember you in all the years to be,
           Know, gray among ghosts in that twilight world,
           That, offered the roses of Pieria, you refused,
           And wander forever in the dark lord Aida's house
           Reticent still, with the blind dead, unknown.

7   [   ] at the temple [   ]
           [   ] thickest [   ]
           And you O Dika weave with your slender hands
           A crown of flowers and dill into those lovely curls,
           For she comes first before the serendipitous Graces
           Who comes in flowers. The uncrowned they turn away.

8   Spring
           Too long
           Gongyla

           Is there any sign from the oracle
           To the girls most of all
           Hermes, at least, has entered my dreams

           I said, O Lord
           Not, I swear, by the blessed goddess
           None can be pleased by that impending

But if ever any longed to die
To see the lotos heavy under dew
On the banks of Acheron

9   I've fouled the weft, the warp, and the shuttle,
Mother my sweet, bewildered by love, by that boy,
And by the slender Aphródita.

10   Why, after so long, should I dream
Of those girlish days?

11   The little girls
Wove crowns
Of leaves.

12   Asleep against the breasts of a friend.

13   The gods [   ] tears [   ]
[   ].

I

14   Crying Asia! that famous place,
The messenger came from his dust.
Crying Ektor! the winded runner
Silver with sweat, laughing, Ektor!
Ektor comes from that famous Asia,
From its strange towns with his friends.
They bring home a black-eyed girl
From Theba the high on the Plakia,
The graceful, the young Andrómakha.
They come in the ships on the ocean.
For gifts they bring wrist-chains of gold,

And purple coats and silver jars,
And carved toys incredibly strange,
And things made of ivory.

II

So the runner said.
                              Quick with astonishment,
Ektor's father shouted for his friends,
And told the coming the city over.
Ilos' boys put wheels to the high carts
And hitched the mules. Wives and girls
Came to stand with Priam's daughters.
Bachelors led the chariot horses;
Charioteers like gods sang commands.

III

A long parade sings its way from the sea.
The flutes are keen and the drums tight;
Charmed air holds the young girls' songs.
Along the way the people bring them bowls
Of cassia, cups of olibanum and myrrh.
Dancing grandmothers shout the marriage song.
Men and boys march and sing to Páon,
To Apollo of the harp, archer of archers,
And sing that Ektor and Andrómakha
Are like two of the gods together.

15   Desire has shaken my mind
             As wind in the mountain forests
             Roars through trees.

16   You were to me then a shy little girl.

17   Who is this wild girl with the charm
           To get you under her spell? [
           [   ] She's always
           In a country frock [
           Too ignorant to arrange her dress
           So that the hem is at the ankle.

18   With eyes like that, stand still,
           Gaze with candor from that beauty,
           Bold as friends before each other.

19   Swallow, swallow,
           Pandion's daughter
           Of wind and sky,
           Why me, why me?

20   He seems to be a god, that man
           Facing you, who leans to be close,
           Smiles, and, alert and glad, listens
           To your mellow voice

           And quickens in love at your laughter
           That stings my breasts, jolts my heart
           If I dare the shock of a glance.
           I cannot speak,

           My tongue sticks to my dry mouth,
           Thin fire spreads beneath my skin,
           My eyes cannot see and my aching ears
           Roar in their labyrinths.

           Chill sweat slides down my body,
           I shake, I turn greener than grass.
           I am neither living nor dead and cry
           From the narrow between.

But endure, even this grief of love.

21   Down from the blue sky
           Came Eros taking off his clothes,
           His shirt of Phoenician red.

22   The word went around
                   [And]rome[da] was forgotten
           Rites and games in their seasons
           Sappho O we loved you

           To the Queen in Kypros
           Tall in our certainty
           Daylight was in those eyes
           Famous in every ear

           Young beyond Acheron.

23   If only they had woven me such luck,
           Aphródita crowned with golden leaves,
           When my cloth was on the loom.

24   [   ]
           [   ] that labor [   ]
           [   ].

           [   ] to sing [   ]
           [   ] a storm wind [   ]
           [   ] and no pain [   ]

           [   ] I urge [   ]
           Gongyla[   ]harp
           [   ]whose longing again
           Hovers on wings

Around your loveliness. For when she sees
The long pleats of your dress in their moving
She catches her breath at the beauty,
And I laugh for joy.

Goddess born from the sea at Kypros
Thus I pray [   ]
That [   ]
I long [   ].

I

25   A company of horsemen or of infantry
Or a fleet of ships, some say,
Is the black earth's finest sight,
But to me it is what you love.

This can be understood in its round truth
By all, clearly, for she who in her beauty
Surpassed all mankind, Elena, left her husband,
The best of men,

And sailed to Troia, mindless of her daughter,
And of her parents whom she loved.
But [   ]
[   ] led her astray.

[   ]
[   ] lightness in her heart [   ]
That I remember Anaktoria now
So far away.

I would rather see the fetching way she walks
And the smiling brightness of her eyes
Than the chariots and charioteers of Lydia
In full armor charging.

[   ] cannot become
[   ] man [   ] approach with sacrifice and pray

[   ]
[   ].

II

Handsome horses O shiver and admire,
Long ships and symmetries of archers,
But black earth's fine sight for me
Is her I love.

Heart's hunger all can understand.
Did not she up and leave the best of men,
Helen that beautifulest of womankind?
[   ]

And forgot her kin and forgot her children
To follow however far into whatever luck
The wild hitherward of her headlong heart
[   ]

[   ]
[   ]
Anaktoria so far away, remember me,
Remember me, who had rather

Hear the melody of your walking
And see the torch-flare of your smile
Than the long battleline of Lydia's charioteers,
Round shields and helmets.

26   And there, when they had stirred
The magic liquor in the jug,
And Ermais, in each held out cup
Had poured from a leather bottle
Every god his ambrosia,
Each tipped some out, for piety,

And rang his cup against another,
That all bright and noble things
Come to our new kinsman.

27   Sweetpeas flowered golden
All over the marsh.

28   Too much is enough
Of that girl Gorgo.

29   Air
Bound
Cu[p
Mus[lin
Forth[with
Of sleep
[*five lines
  indecipherable*]
Beautiful
Fluttering
[   ] ivory
Cl[asp.

30   They wore red yarn to bind their hair,
Our girls when they were young,
This, or no finery at all.

That, to be grand [
But those labyrinthine curls of yours,
Yellower than [

Great overhanging hat of leaves
And the fattest of flowers,
With a snug and perfect snood

Embroidered, Persian, and from Sardis,
That [   ] city
[   ]

And Kleïs, I do not have for you
That rich embroidered snood
That you want, but in Mytilena [

[   ]
Girls   [   ] to have [
If the embroidered

These Kleanaktida [
You flee [
These memories. Know that our name is gone.

31   Bride with beautiful feet.

32   Though you are my lover,
             Take for wife a younger woman;
             Find a newer bed to lie in,
             I could not bear to be the older.

33   Dusk and western star,
             You gather
             What glittering sunrise
             Scattered far,
             The ewe to fold,
             Kid and nanny home,
             But the daughter
             You send wandering
             From her mother.

             [   ]
             Hesperos, most beautiful
             Of stars.

34   And your boy's beauty,
           What else is so trim, so lithe,
           Impetuous follower?
           Straight slender trees
           Have that balance.

35   [   ]
           silent, still
           the holy goatskin wearing
           Kytherean, I am praying
           she who owns my mind
           hear my prayers, so high
           she who has left me behind
           against me green
           harsh [

36   Never, Irana, have I met anybody
           More bothersome than you.

                                    I

37   With quickened heart they hovered,
           Fluttered, and lit with folding wings,
           The doves. My heart is cold.

                                    II

           Their wings fold down,
           My heart grows chill.

38   Loving girls more than Gello.

39   She had others at Kytherea to nurse her,
           But Peitho, they say, is the daughter of Aphródita

[   ]
A gift for honor [
And Gyrinno [
[   ]
But never say that [
Beautifully you speak [
[   ]
The west wind blows upon me
[   ]
Sliding across the air
            on wings spread wide
[   ]
She writes these matters to Andromeda.

40   She was like that sweetest apple
            That ripened highest on the tree,
            That the harvesters couldn't reach,
            And pretended they forgot.
            [   ]
            Like the mountain hyacinth trod underfoot
            By shepherd men, its flower purple on the ground.

41   Wrapped up in rich shaggy wool.

42   [   ] of Eros, anxious [   ]
            [   ]
            [   ] I admire, I gaze at you [   ]
            [   ]Ermiona herself, as like her
            [   ] you are as blonde as Elena,
            [decorous, suave.]
            [   ] to mortal women, but know this
            [   ]me[   ] all solicitude
            [   ] but
            [   ]
            [   ] dew on the riverside gleaming

[   ]
[   ] to make it last all night long.

43   [   ] Sard[is   ]
How many times she must remember us here
Where once [   ] we [   ]
She had divinity in her.

Her dancing, of all, was your enchantment.
And now she moves among the Lydian ladies
As when the sun has set and the stars come out
And the rose red moon

Lifts into the midst of their pale brightness.
Her light is everywhere, on the salt-bitter sea,
On fields thick and rich with flowers
And beautiful under dew,

On roses, tangled parsley, and the honey-headed clover.
Her light is everywhere, remembering
Atthis in her young sweetness, desiring her
With tender, heavy heart.

There, in that far place, that we come [
Knows not [   ] many
Hears [   ] the between
[   ].

They are not mine, the deerhide shoes of Asia,
That body to hold, with its goddess's beauty
To have against [
[   ].

Soft [   ] Eros
And [   ] Aphródita
[   ] nectar poured into
Golden [   ].

[   ] enticement with her hands
[
[
[   ].

[   ] in the month of Geraistios
[   ] lovers
[   ] never
[   ] I shall come.

44   They gave me honor,
          The gift of their skill.

45   Her shoes were leather and from Asia,
          Rich Lydian patterns across the toes.

46   [   ] Mika
          [   ] I shall not let you
          You have taken Penthilea for your sweetheart,
          Treating me with less than kindness
          [   ] and a song, sweet
          [   ] with low, gentle voice
          [   ] crystal clarity in that song
          [   ] dewfall upon the world.

47   Came husband,
                  mischief,
          ]ing bri[ght]

48   Don't stir
          The trash.

49   Where do the butler's big feet go?
Fourteen yards from heel to toe!
Five red oxen gladly died,
Ten frantic cobblers stitched the hide,
That stylish slippers trim and neat
Besplendor those important feet.

50   High in the chariot,
As when the mastersinger of Lesbos
Against all the outlanders.

51   Violet breasted daughter of Kronos.

52   As once in Crete,
A round dance of girls
In that antique time.

53   She taught the champion runner,
Hero of Gyara.

54   Arkheanassa and Gorgo
Sleep together as married folk,
Wherefore she is called her wife.
And Pleistodiké, she was her wife
In between Gongyla and Gorgo.
They've given themselves a name
Together and [   ] Pleistodiké
[   ] shall be known as
[   ].

55   With that island-born
Holiness of Kypros

I talked; she talked,
And all in a dream.

56   Now that Andromeda has her fair reply
           [   ]
           Psappho, why Aphródita of so many pleasures?

57   All yellow gold and like a daughter,
           A flower, that girl, with a flower's beauty,
           And, Kleïs, not for all the girls in Lydia,
           My word of honor on our friendship,
           Nor for all the Mytilenian virgins,
           Would I leave her.

58   [   ]
           For the sake of the old
           [   ]
           Voice [   ]
           Before [   ].

59   And then [   ]
           Not even one [   ]
           And now]   ]
           Nor wishes [   ]
           Mnasidika is more beautiful of body
           Than the svelte Gyrinno.

60   Rose
           [   ]
           Speak
           [   ]
           Yearning

[   ]
Sweat.

I

61   Brightness and [
[   ]
    with luck in the outcome
        overcomes
          black
[   ]
   sailors
        high winds
         and on shore
[   ]
   sails
       the cargo
[   ]
    streaming, many
[   ]
   work
       of the land
[   ].

II

Pray now the women
       At Demeter's altar
Prophecies, songs,
      brightness and
[   ]
Fortunate and well-bred together
    crushes, crashes
These black ships
Haul in and batten, the sailors,
High seas, heavy weather, gales,
Reefs and land off port

[   ]
        far more than
                the cargo shifting
              oarlocks awash, waves
[   ]
      many that
[   ]
        desperation,
      land
[   ].

62   Aphródita
        delightful words
        may throw
        holding
        sits
        [   ]
        seafoam.

63   For Aphródita, this purple handkerchief
        To wear on her head against the heat,
        An honored gift from Phokaia.

64   O there are no others like her,
        Not in these times, lover.

I

65   Percussion, salt and honey,
        A quivering in the thighs;
        He shakes me all over again,
        Eros who cannot be thrown,
        Who stalks on all fours
        Like a beast.

II

Eros makes me shiver again
Strengthless in the knees,
Eros gall and honey,
Snake-sly, invincible.

66   You hate me who loves you, Atthis,
And flutter around Andromeda.

67   O Pollyanna
Polyanaktidas,
Good-bye, good-bye.

68   Golden goblets with knucklebone stems.

69   I am Aphródita of the shifting eyes.
My servants are Eros and you, my Sappho.

70   *The scholar Aristides, pondering*
material and spiritual wealth,
recalls that Sappho in a poem said:

The Muses have made me happy
And worthy of the world's envy,
So that even beyond death
I shall be remembered.

71   [   ] downward my tears [   ]
Let trouble come to sting the whipper
And a high wind blow him away.

72   And I yearn
           And I hunt.

73   The stars around the moon in her beauty
           Dim their bright patterns of fire
           When her light is full upon the world.

           The Emperor Julian, quoting Sappho in a letter,
           remembered these lines as:

           When the moon is silver
           She hides the stars around her
           From our sight.

74   Daughter of kings
           The sons of kings,
           Hail!

I

75   Leave your siege of her violet softness.
           The night is long and we shall sing
           Epithalamia outside your door.

           Call to your bachelor friends to come.
           All night long, like the nightingale,
           We shall stay awake and sing.

II

           The night is long but girls will sing
           Songs all night outside your door
           To keep you from her violet softness.

           Leave her alone! Go back to your friends,
           Or all night long, like nightingales,
           We shall stay awake and sing.

76   For even then, when you were a little girl,
              Come on! you said, *let's sing to your lyre*
              [   ]
              [   ] you were never far from me,
              A wonder of gracefulness.

              And now we walk to a wedding,
              Beautifully you [
              [   ] send the girls quickly
              [   ] might have
              [   ] the road to high Olympos
              [   ] men [   ].

77   [   ] all too often [   ]
              [   ] because those I do the most for
              Hurt me the worst
              [   ] idle [
              [   ] on the knees
              [   ]
              [   ]
              [   ] you, I am willing]
              [   ]suffering[
              [   ] and I, for myself [
              This I knew something about
              [   ] for them [

78   Before my lying heart could speak for life
              I longed for death. Misery the size of terror
              Was in her tears when we unclasped forever.
              Sappho! she cried,

              That I could stay! Joy goes with you, I said,
              Remember what has been, the rose-and-violet crowns
              I wove into your hair when we stood so close together,
              Heart against heart,

              The garlands I plaited of flower with flower
              Around your graceful neck, the oils of spices

As precious as for a queen [
[   ].

Deep in the cushions on that softest bed
Where, free in desire [
[   ] tender lovers
[   ].

None [   ] holy, and no [
There was, that we were apart from [
No sacred grove [
[   ].

79   First news of springtime,
          The lovesong of the nightingale.

80   I have neither the honey nor the bee.

81   Haughtier than a horse.

82   And let her find you, Kyprian, bitterer still,
          To keep her loud tongue from saying ever
          That Eros hot and flustering came to Dorikha
          A second time.

83   [   ]
          around
          you, Atthis
          clouds
          [   ]

84   of Dorikha
                  called, and no

[   ]
reaches to, arrogant of heart
to be half asleep with love
[   ].

85   Heart
           altogether
           I can
           [   ]
           may be for me
           throws back the light
           [hand]some face
           [   ]
           caressed
           [   ]

86   Staying
           in the burnt offering
           her, holding the finest

           and she, walking
           for we saw
           of the work
           [   ]
           and back again
           [   ]
           to say this

87   [   ]
           Graces
           [   ]
           you, at least
           [   ].

88   Shall give
no matter what
the beautiful and the splendid
you may grieve
my disgrace
rising, on
were you pained
not this way
is [she] inclined
nor yet
       I understand
           the worst man of all
[   ]
    to the others
       the mind
           luck-
[   ].

89   [   ]
not even
lovely
[   ]
flower
longing
pleased
[   ].

90   Someone, I'm bold to say,
Will remember us
In time hereafter.

91   Wealth without moral splendor
Makes a dangerous neighbor;
But join the two together:
There is no higher fortune.

92   Sometimes she closed her eyes
              All night long.

93   Far more melodious than the harp,
              More golden than gold.

94   Lady Dawn.

95   When fury rages in the breast,
              Watch that reiterating tongue.

96   Softer than a fine dress.

97   These pleasures now, my constant girls,
              I shall sing in splendid songs.

98   While they kept watch around her
              [   ] the bridegrooms
              [   ] lords of the town.

99   To whose eyes?

100   Eros weaver of myths,
              Eros sweet and bitter,
              Eros bringer of pain.

                          I

101   [   ] slick with slime [   ]
              [   ] Polyanaktidas to satiety [   ]

[   ] shoots forward [   ]
Playing such music upon these strings
Wearing a phallus of leather [   ]
Such a thing as this [   ] enviously
[   ] twirls quivering masterfully
[   ] and has for odor
[   ] hollow [   ]
[   ]
[   ] mysteries, orgies
[   ] leaving
[   ]an oracle
[   ] comes [   ]
[   ]
[com]panions
[mys]teries
[   ]
[   ]
[   ]sister
So [   ]
[   ] wishes [   ]
Displays again Polyanaktidas [   ]
This randy madness I joyfully proclaim.

II

[   ]
Her [
Man [
And see[ms
These girls al[l
Topmost [
Wanders [
[   ] these [
[   ]
Partner [
Own cousin [
Elbows [
Laughing away [

This [
The [
Cries O [
Blood [
Sharp [
[   ]
[   ]
Well [
Shall please again [
And from [
O girls [
[   ].

I

102   Raise the ridge-pole higher, higher,
O marriage night O binding god
Carpenters! Make the roof-tree taller,
O marriage night O binding god
He comes, the husband, and walks like Ares,
O marriage night O binding god
He's taller by far than a tall man,
O marriage night O binding god

II

Pitch the roof-beam higher, builders.
O hymn Hymen, high men, O!
Joiners! The roof is far too low.
O hymn Hymen high, men O!
He stands, the husband, as long as Ares,
O hymn high Hymen, men O!
And he can't get it through the door.

103   Mermaids and you brine-born on the Kypros sand,
Bring back my brother over your sea unhurt,
That his wandering heart have for its own
Its real desire.

Wash off all that wrong upon his head;
Make him a brightness to those who love him
[   ] to his enemies a distress,
And let none hereafter [

Let him be willing to do honor to his sister
[   ] and the miserable sorrows
[   ] grieving as we did before
[   ]

[   ] hearing the [   ] of the millet,
Townspeople murmuring in the marketplace
[   ] and again no
[   ]

[   ]
[   ] and you Kyprian [   ]
[   ] put away the evil [   ]
[   ].

104   Kyprian and sea-daughters of Nereos,
            Grant to my brother that he come here
            Unharmed, and that all the wishes in his heart
            Come to be fulfilled,

            Let him be washed clean before the gods,
            That he be a delight to all who love him.

105   Near me [
            Lady Era [
            Their praying, the princes of Atreos [
            The kings [

            Brought to its end [
            From the beginning around [
            At a loss for their passage here [
            They could not.

Till you and Zeus [
And of Thyona the love[ly
And now [
In the manner of old [

The pure and chaste [
Girls [
Around [
[   ].

I

106   Stand beside me, worshiped Hera, strange in a dream,
Ghost or visitation but in a shape all grace,
Sudden as before the famous Mycenaean kings
When they cried out

At the awful end of pulling Troy to the ground,
Their ships turned homeward down the rapid
    Skamander,
And knew that lest you guide them they were luckless,
And prayed your love,

And called to strongest Zeus and Thyona's son
The cherished. Like them, lady queen, I ask
To return to my country, homecoming with your
Benediction,

That among the virgins of Mytilene, as before,
I perform the chaste and holy rites in splendor,
And teach the dances and make songs for the holy days.
O bring me home.

II

Before me, Potni' Era, appear to mortal eyes,
Clear in body, beautiful, bright,

As when the far-sung Atridaean princes
Stood, as I, in prayer:

Who fought so hard at Ilion's wall,
Wandered so long over all the sea,
Lost, after so much labor and death,
Helpless to return

Until they cried to you, to Zeus Antiaos,
And to Thyona's darling son, their prayer.
Treat me now in those ancient ways,
Bring grace upon me.

The chaste [
virgins [
Around [
[   ].

107   Whether you are at Kypros and Paphos
            Or at Panormos.

108   You make me hot.

109   I gave you a white goat.

110   [   ]
                        beautiful
                    peace become havoc
                    weariness of heart
                    sits down against
                    but up, O friends
                    for day is nigh
            [   ]

111   Until all of you are willing.

112   You have come, and done,
                 And I was waiting for you
                 To temper the red desire
                 That burned my heart.

113   Beauty is for the eyes and fades in a while,
                 But goodness is a beauty that lasts forever.

114   I don't know which way I'm running.
                 My mind is part this way, part that.

115   ] come forward, tell [

116   Bridegroom, exult! Just as you prayed,
                 The rites are done and you are married.
                 The girl, just as you prayed, is yours.
                 [   ].
                 All gracefulness your body and your eyes
                 [   ]
                 Softly Eros rises in your longing face
                 [   ]
                 Aphródita has honored you above all.

117   Wet handkerchief.

118   ALKAIOS
                 I have something I'm willing to tell you,
                 But bashfulness holds me back.

SAPPHO
If your heart is for the noble and beautiful
And your tongue is free of all things ugly,
Reticence need not lower your eyes:
Speak out whatever is fitting and right.

119   [
               [
               [Her] shirt
               Yel[low]
               [Her] petticoat
               And splendor
               Radiant yellow
               [Her] red dress
               Robes the color of peaches
               Peach-flower crowns
               Pretty eyes
               Phrygian
               Red
               Carpet
               [
               P[

120   Dawn with small golden feet.

121   *Parthenia, parthenia,*
               poi me lipois' apoikhe?
               Girlhood O girlhood,
               Lost of a sudden,
               Where have you gone?

               Ouketi exo
               pros se
               ouket' exo,
               Nowhere, bride my darling,
               Nowhere near you.

122   ]him[
            [   ]
            ]becomes[

123   Black dreams of such virulence[
            That sleep's sweetness[
            And terrible grief[
            This place is religious[
            Happiness, no, and hope neither[
            And I indeed am so[
            Delightful the games[
            And I[
            This[

124   There are none like her,
            And none will ever see the light of the sun,
            None hereafter will have that mastery.

            Or, to accommodate another meaning of sophia:

            I cannot believe there is any girl
            Under the sun, or shall be to come,
            With an intelligence like hers.

125   ] curls [   ] placing the lyre.

126   ] bridegroom, for your tiresome bachelor friends

127   [   ]
                        toward
            [
                        should you be willing
                        few

to be borne
any
regard that pleasure
you know and
have forgotten but grief

[

if any speak
for I also
no longer than to the day after tomorrow
to be loved
love, I say, will become strong

[

and grievous
sharp

[

and know this
whoever you
will love

[
[

of the arrows

[   ].

128   Clear keen song.

129   *A phrase remembered by Aristides*
           when he was talking about the clear
           light of Smyrna:

           Brightness that strikes the eyes

130   O beautiful, O graceful

131   When songs from the heart.

132 When she, the round moon, rose,
They stood in a ring around her altar.

133 To Gyrinno.

134 I put here, my lazy girl, this soft cushion,
And if, with your blouse off, in your soft arms.

135 Pure and holy Graces and Muses who live at Pieria

136 Place there the nature of the violet breasted.

137 Slender Graces and Muses with beautiful hair,
Come hither, come now.

138 He is dying, Kytherea,
The young Adonis,
What can we put around him?

Beat your breasts, girls,
Tear your dresses.

139 [   ]
all
and the other
[   ]

140 More valuable than gold.

141   is fragrant
       [*five lines indecipherable*]
       walk
       so I saw
       [   ]
       lady
       golden
       [   ]
       heart
       [   ].

142   Those discords,
       I don't think,
       Will reach the sky.

143   Seven ways in terror,
              the laurel tree,
                    a forest all of pine,
       The empty,
       And these
                    the wayfarer
       As the mouse, silent, hidden,
       O girlish heart,
              a mind so calm that
       Comes with kisses and open arms
       Seven
              her beauty
       Is.

144   [   ]
       pretty
       Artemis
       [   ].

145   You too, Kalliopa,
              Yourself.

146   ] called you
                            ] filled your mouth with plenty
                            ] girls, fine gifts
                            ] lovesong, the keen-toned harp
                            ] an old woman's flesh
                            ] hair that used to be black
                            ] knees will not hold
                            ] stand like dappled fawns
                              ] but what could I do?
                            ] no longer able to begin again
                              ] rosy armed Dawn
                                ] bearing to the ends of the earth
                                  ] nevertheless seized
                                  ] the cherished wife
                                  ] withering is common to all
                                  ] may that girl come and be my lover
              I have loved all graceful things [   ] and this
              Eros has given me, beauty and the light of the sun.

147   I am willing.

148   Once upon a time, the story goes,
              Leda found a hyacinthine egg.

149   Tenderer than the rose.

150   A coronet of celery.

151   To die is evil.
The gods think so,
Else they would die.

152   Hail, bride!
Hail, honored bridegroom!
Long life!

153   More harmonious than lyres.

154   [   ]
loves
[   ].

155   [as it happens
] wishes, being childless still
] I see the fulfilment
] I summoned
] all of a sudden against my heart
] as much as you wish it to come about
] to struggle against me
] is voluptuous in her enticement
] but you know well

156   It is not fitting to mourn the dead
In a house where the Muses are served.
Let us have no mourning here.

157   Muses, come down again,
Leaving that golden [

158   Weaker than water.

159   [   ]
               [   ]
               The festival
               [   ]

160   Eros, child of Gea and Ouranos.

161   Whiter than milk.

162   The goddess Persuasion,
               Daughter of Aphródita.

163   Medeia.

164   Lato and Nioba were very loving friends.

165   All colors tangled together.

166   We shall give, Father said.

167   me away from them
               and we became
               like the gods
               against the gods
               Andromeda
               [   ]

no longer unstained
Tyndarides
with grace
honest no more with
the great palaces
[   ]
the doors
in a fury
the guard corporal
wrestling
[   ]

168   And night's black sleep upon the eyes.

169   Your darling.

170   With the bride that happy,
            Let the bridegroom rejoice.

171   Of the Muses.

172   Whiter by far than an egg.

173   [   ] I
            [   ]
            [   ]
            I hold the quince [
              ] of the little girls.

174   The island Aiga.

175   Barbitos, Baromos, Barmos.

176   As good natured as a little girl,
               I don't snap and pout and rage.

177   The dress.

178   [   ]
                    here
               [   ]
                    again
               [   ]

179   She calls her daughter.

180   A girl picking a flower just opened.

181   ] above[
               ] you shall remember[
               ] in our girlhood[
               ] we made[
               ] for and[
               ] the town-[
               [*several lines gone*]
               ] facing[
               [   ]
               ] endurance[
                       ]man[
               [   ]
                     ]all[

182   Handbag.

183   Falling downward.

184   Ektor.

185   All that's [loved]
           Tell [
           Tongue [
           Mythology [
           And to men [
           Larger [

186   And this [
           Grief from the divine powers [

           Surely [   ] did not love [
           And now because [

           And the responsibility [
           Nor many [

187   Became [
           For no [

188   Gentle of voice.

           *Or, considering
           the scribe's spelling:*

           With honey in her words.

189   [   ]
chtho[nic   ]
[   ]

190   Vines trellised on poles.

191   I might lead.

192   [   ]
and I go
[   ]
and surely you failed
harmony
the dance
[   ]

193   That man seems to her.

194   Trench for watering the garden.

195   Danger.

196   Wise in many things.

197   Soda.

198   Without guile.

199   I wish to go.

200   [   ]
anointing
[   ]
forgetfulness
[   ]
bedroom

201   Ford at the river.

202   [   ]
peers
[   ]
of children
[   ]
[*several*
  indecipherable
  lines]

gods
shameful
[   ]

203   O Adonis!

204   Dawn.

205   The girl with the pleasing voice.

206   You have begun to forget me [
      ] or do you love some other?

207   Just when dawn in her golden sandals.

208   beforehand
                 to carry
                 and willing
                 Arkheanassa
                 whenever in dreams
                 the softball umpire
                 fell in love

                 [   ]
                 receive
                 [   ]

                 [   ]
                 upon
                 speech[less
                 [   ]

                 [   ]
                 heard
                 Kran[n]iades
                 girls
                 [   ]

209   Done [
                 Compassion [
                 Trembling [
                 [   ]
                 [   ] old age and wrinkles so soon [
                 Wanders around [
                 [   ] flies in pursuit [
                 [   ]
                 Of the noble [

[   ] she, taking [
[   ] sang to us
The violet-breasted [
[   ]
[   ] most of all [
[   ] the wandering [

210   Lead off, my lyre,
               And we shall sing together.

211   Growing old [
               By Gongyla, close [
               Apples [
               [   ] acorns [
               [   ] and Sappho
               She [
               [   ] hearts [
               [   ] Kalliope [
               Feel

212   All a lively summer [
               On the run [
               [   ] and she a child
               Playing in country quiet
               Country games and games
               They play in Ionia [
               [   ] too.
               And so many city people [
               [   ] together there [
               That Kallias the Mytilenian
               Said in [
               [   ] Aphrodi-
               ta.

I

213   The moon has set, and the Pleiades.
It is the middle of the night,
Hour follows hour. I lie alone.

II

The moon has gone
To her Endymion,
The Pleiades
Their seven lovers please.

Since Esperos glistened
And the moon rose red,
I have listened
Alone in my bed.

ALKMAN

1. A Hymn to Artemis of the Strict Observance

For a Chorus of Spartan Girls Dressed as Doves
To Sing at Dawn on the Feast of the Plow

I

1

[   ]
[   ]
[   ]
[   ]
[   ]
[   ]
[   ]
[   ] Polydeukes.
I cannot find Lykaithos among the dead
Enarsphoros and with him the fast runner Thebros
[   ] the violent
[   ] the helmeted
And Euteikhes and the lord of lands Areios
[   ] mightiest of men half gods.

2

[   ] the hunter
[   ] the great and Eurytos
[   ] blind tumult
[   ] most brave

[   ] we shall [not] go across
[   ] Destiny and Providence
[   ] the oldest of all the gods
[   ] force goes barefoot
A wild heart must not crowd divinity
Nor rush upon Aphrodite hot to marry
[   ] Wanassa, nor any
[   ] Porkos' daughter
[   ] Graces from the house of Zeus
[   ] eyes all love in their looking.

3   [   ] Fate
        [   ] to friends
        [   ] gave gifts
        [   ]
        [   ] destroyed youth
        [   ]
        [   ]
        [   ] left, the one by an arrow
        [   ] marble millstone
        [   ] to Hades
        [   ] they
        [   ] are unforgotten
Who suffered the evil their own hands made.

4   And there is the vengeance of the gods.
        He is a happy man who can weave his days,
        No trouble upon the loom.
        And I, I sing of Agido,
        Of her light. She is like the sun
        To which she makes our prayers,
        The witness of its radiance.
        Yet I can neither praise her nor blame her
        Till I have sung of another,
        Sung of our choirmaster,
        Who stands among us as in a pasture
        One splendid stallion

Paws the meadow, a champion racer,
A horse that runs in dreams.

5   Imagine her if you can. Her hair,
As gold as a Venetian mane,
Flowers around her silver eyes.
What can I say to make you see?
She is Hagesikhora and
Agido, almost, almost as beautiful,
Is a Kolaxaian filly running behind her
In the races at Ibeno.
A Pleiades of doves they are
Contending at dawn before the altar of Artemis
For the honor of offering the sacred plow
Which we have brought to the goddess.
They are the white star Sirius rising
In the honey and spice of a summer night.

6   Neither abundance of purple
Can defend us with its glory,
Nor golden snakes engraved with eyes and scales,
Nor bonnets from Lydia and brooches,
Nor our sweet violet eyes.
Nor can Nanno's hair, Areta's goddess face,
Thylakis nor Kleësithera,
Nor Ainesimbrota to whom we cry
Let Astaphis be ours,
Let Philylla look our way sometimes,
Damareta and the lovely Wianthemis,
Keep back defeat unless
Hagesikhora alone, our love,
Be our victory's shield.

7   And she is, she is our own,
The splendid-ankled Hagesikhora!

With Agido, by whose side she lingers,
She honors the rites with her beauty.
Accept her prayers O gods,
For she is your handiwork,
Perfect of her kind.
And I, I, O Choirmaster,
Am but an ordinary girl.
I hoot like an owl in the roof.
I long to worship the goddess of the dawn
Whose gift is peace. For Hagesikhora
We sing, for her we virgin girls
Make our lovely harmonies.

8   To the swift trace-horse
             So [   ]
             [   ] to the pilot
             And the ship [   ]
             More melodious than the Sirens
             For they are goddesses. There are ten
             Of us, eleven of them [   ]
             Sings [   ] upon the Yellow River
             The swan. And she of the lovely yellow hair
             [   ]
             [   ]
             [   ]
             [   ]
             [   ].

                            II

4   Vendettas end among the gods.
             Serenity's against the odds.
             But weave and anguish is your thread.
             Agido's light I sing instead,
             Which is the sun's, and she our sun;
             They shine, we cannot tell which one.
             And yet I must not praise her so:

One lovelier than Agido
Must have first praise. Choirmaster, she,
Dazzling as when a stallion, he
Runs beside his stateliest mare,
Outshines us all, O no compare!
A race-horse, she, a champion blood
Long-tailed Paphlagonian stud.

5   See how her hair, so thick, so bold,
A long mane of Venetian gold,
Flowers around her silver face.
What figured image can I place
That Hagesikhora shall stand
As if you touched her with your hand?
I'll keep the horse. Then Agido,
Less beautiful, but scarcely so,
A Colassaian filly seems,
Behind her runs and like her gleams
In the Ibenian races. Or
A Pleiades of doves they are,
Or Sirius rising to light
The honeydark sweet summer night.

6   Hold O Sidonian red our wall.
With wrists snakebound we stand or fall.
Our golden, written serpents stare,
Lydian bright bands bind our hair.
We stand, contending, jeweled girls,
Unarmed except by Nanno's curls.
Armed with but our violet eyes,
Ainesimbrota's beauty vies,
That Philylla loves, and Thyakis,
Damareta and Astaphis,
Wianthemis the randy, too,
Klesithera, Areta who
Is like a god, but silver-heeled
Hagesikhora is our shield.

7   Is Hagesikhora our own,
         So elegant of anklebone?
         As faithful as to Agido!
         The gods we could not honor so
         But that, O gods, you love her too.
         What you mean humankind to do
         She does, and brings perfection home,
         While I, who sing by metronome,
         Ordinary and unaloof,
         Hoot like an owl in the roof.
         When on Aoti's A we pitch
         How flat the Doric counterstitch
         O Hagesikhora, unless
         You join the ringing loveliness.

                            III

Oionos, grayhound lean, dove-gray of eye,
Herakles' mother Alkmena's brother Likymnios' son,
Came, Artemis bound and looking upon the world
With the broad-backed hero to Sparta's invisible wall,
Came, fought the watchdog of Hippokoön, and under
The walking sticks of Hippokoön's sons died.
A summer storm his anger black with thunder Herakles
Struck the Hippokoönta as lightning hits a mountain.
His hands were terror when he struck, and hell his eyes.

Struck and retreated, the bite of a knife in his hand.
But before the sun had changed his gate again,
He came shouting back with a squadron of soldiers.
Ruled thereafter over the house of Hippokoön
Persephoneia, bride of the lord of the dead.
For they had vied before with Kastor and Polydeukes;
Enasphoros with Helen, a family against Tyndareus.
It is not wise, it is unmeasured, to bait divinity
With common hands, to scale Olympos wild of heart.

There fell Enarsphoros the breeder of horses,
Thebros the swift, victor of races in armor,
Euteikhes, and the lord of lands Areios,
Tall, bold sons, mightiest of men half gods.
Eurytos and Lykaithos crossed into Hades,
Returning to fate the debt of existence.
Vengeance, vengeance, and the hand of the gods.
Life is not woven without grief on the loom.
Grace, grace is not from humankind.

For peace we cry O Artemis the grandmother of lions,
Nurse of hedgehogs and fawns, white-breasted dawn!
To the fading stars we sing, we sing our Agido
The doe-slight, slender cousin of Hagesikhora the tall.
She is so like the sun that when she lifts her rosy arms,
Which is Helios, which Agido? But Hagesikhora
Among us is like a stallion among his mares,
The silken quiver of his flanks rounding their eyes,
A horse from a dream and not of this world.

The manes of the haughty Venetian horses
Are like her hair, streaming water combed by the wind.
Her eyes are silver from the time of Tiryns,
And yet all my words are wide of her beauty.
If Agido is a yearling from Kolaxaia,
She is a racer from Ibeno. They are Sirius,
They are the wheeling doves of the Pleiades,
They are the bearers of the holy plow of the goddess
In the half-light of the night-sweet dawn.

There is not insolence enough of purple among us
To back the contending chorus from the altar,
Nor snakes upon our arms, solid gold with godly eyes,
Nor Lydian hats nor gems nor porphyry in our gaze.
Nanno's hair cannot defend us, nor Areta's pretty face,
Nor Thylakis or Kleësithera or Ainesimbrota,
Philylla, Wianthemis, Darareta, Astaphis.

None, none shall bring us to our triumph
Unless the lovely Hagesikhora lead the dance.

She leads, she and Agido; their ankles are the dance.
Listen, gods, to their hymn, for none is more beautiful.
Beside their singing my song is an owl's hoo!
I sing for them as they sing for the goddess,
And all for peace, till all at last is one harmony.
Come, dawn, as to the trumpeting swans of Sparta,
As day finds the Sirens at their song.
Feed us, earth and heart and grace of peace;
Beauty, beauty, like that tossing yellow hair.

IV

1   [   ] Polydeukes.
I do not find Lykaithos
among the dead.
Enarsphoros, Thebros swiftfoot.
The violent, the helmeted.
Euteikhes, king Areion
[   ] strong
men, half gods.

2   [   ] the hunter.
Eurytos. Tumult.
We shall not pass.
Aisa, Poros: Fate, Luck.
These are older
than the gods.
Brutes stalk unshod.
Wild hearts rush not
upon the gods,
nor upon Aphrodite
amorous [   ]
Queen, daughter

of Porkos. Graces
love-eyed [   ]
from Zeus' house.

3   [   ]
          [   ] arrow,
          marble millstone
          [   ]
          suffered evil
          of their own making.

4   There is the god's revenge.
          Happy the man of calm mind
          who weaves his day
          unweeping. But I sing
          the light of Agido: I see
          her as the sun, which she,
          Agido, calls
          to shine, its witness.
          But I may not
          praise or blame her.
          Our mastersinger
          must come first,
          as in a field
          the sleek, galloping
          stallion,
          winner of races,
          stands apart,
          as if seen in a dream.

5   Do you not see her?
          She is a racehorse
          of the Venetii.
          But the hair of my kinswoman
          Hagesikhora is a flower

of unmixed gold.
Her eyes are silver.
Can I describe her?
She is Hagesikhora.
Her beauty is like Agido's
as a race between
Kolaxaian and Ibenian horses,
as the Pleiades and Sirius
contend in the ambrosia
of the night,
as we contend to bring
the plow to the goddess
in the twilit dawn.

6   For we have not purple
enough to defend ourselves,
nor intricate serpents
all gold,
nor caps of Lydia,
nor violet-eyed glances—
girlhood's jewelry—
nor shall Nanno's hair
defend us,
nor Areta goddesslike,
nor Thylakis, nor Kleïsithera,
nor Ainesimbrota to whom we say:
Give us Astaphis,
Let Philylla look this way,
Damareta and lovely Wianthemis.
For Hagesikhora we long.

7   And is not Hagesikhora,
the fine-ankled, ours?
Does not she keep close to Agido?
She honors the feastday.
Hear them, gods,

gods whose ends they fulfill.
O choirmaster,
I am a mere girl,
I sing like the rafter owl,
yet I sing
to welcome the goddess of the dawn,
the queller of pain,
the Hagesikhora has led us
the lovely way to peace.

8   The trace-horse [   ]
          [   ] the pilot
          the ship [   ]
          more sonorous than Sirens
          [   ] who are gods
          against eleven, ten
          sings [   ]
          on Xanthos waters
          the swan [   ]
          lovable blonde [   ]
          [   ]

2. A Hymn to Hera
For a Chorus of Spartan Girls

Around my heart O singing Olympians
[   ] songs
[   ] hears
[   ] of that voice
[   ] a fine song singing
[   ]
Eyes in the honey of sleep half-closed
[   ] take me along, lead me on

Where wildly shall I shake my yellow hair
[   ] my graceful feet.

(lines 11–60 indecipherable)

All go limp when they see her walking,
Unstrung as if by sleep or sudden death,
All empty and delicious in their minds.
But rather than give back my gaze,
Astymeloisa with her crown of leaves
Goes by like a fierce white star that flares
The brighter sliding down the sky,
Like the first green gold of a tree in spring,
Like milkweed down on the wind
[   ]
On long legs striding she walked away,
And in her long wind-tangled virgin hair
The wind-borne grace of Kinyras rode.
[A]stymeloisa against the contenders
[   ] darling would tame
[   ] I choose
[   ] would that, would that silver
[   ]
[   ] could I but see [   ] lovers
But if her gentle hand took mine,
How fast would I fall on my knees before her!

And now [   ] that stubborn girl
To that girl [   ] holding me
[   ] that girl
[   ] grace.

(lines 86–90 are missing)

The Fragments

3   And Kastor and Polydeukes
       The glorious, skilled horsemen,
       Tamers of wild stallions.

4   Eating nectar.

5   You and your two horses.

6   Thus was born the blessed
       Daughter of Glaukos.

7   A. Sing O Muse, sing high and clear
           O polytonal many-voiced Muse,
           Make a new song for girls to sing.
       B. About the towered temple of Therapne.
       C. Waves rolling seaweed to a silent shore.

8   The song I sing
       Begins with Zeus.

9   The Muse sang,
       The clear-tongued Siren.

10   A. And that man, sprawled in such pleasure, is happy.
       B. That man is happy.

11   He was neither a peasant
Nor awkward with fine folk,
Neither born in Thessaly
Nor a shepherd of Erysikhe,
But from Sardis the high.

12   A charming short
Summer dress.

13   Girls scattered helterskelter,
Chickens and hawkshadow.

14   O Father Zeus,
That I had a husband!

15   If I had thought
Of that for us!

16   Just so, our pretty
Little song.

17   Beautifully singing.

18   As many girls as we have,
They all play the zither.

19   She shall play the flute,
We shall sing the song.

20   When I was a woman
Who.

21   I bring with my prayers
This garland of goldflower
And delicious galingale.

22   Not I, O Lady,
O daughter of Zeus.

23   Was it really Apollo
I saw in a dream?

24   May my heart rejoice
In the house of Zeus
And in thine, O lord.

25   Me, O son of Leto,
The leader of your chorus.

26   Long Thrower, son of Zeus,
Muses in their yellow robes.

27   Leaving Kypros the lovely
And Paphos ringed with waves.

28   That is not Aphrodite in the ginger grass
But randy Eros batting flowers.
Touch not! Touch not! he cries.

29   How many times on the mountain tops,
Streaming torches held high for the gods,
Have you brought the great golden jug
As deep as the churns the shepherds use,
Placed it full of lion's milk in the cave,
That its curds change to whitest cheese,
[Bacchante! O Bacchante!]

30   Near the holy cliffs,
Near the island of Psyra.

31   Ino, queen of the sea,
Upon whose breasts.

32   Nourished by Ersa,
Daughter of Zeus
And of holy Selana,
The moon.

33   Sister of Eunomia
And of Peitho,
Daughter of Promathea.

34   One roll of the dice
Stirs up the ghosts.

35   My hearth is cold but the day will come
When a rich pot of red bean soup
Is on the table, the kind Alkman loves,
Good peasant cooking, nothing fine.
The first day of autumn, you shall be my guest.

36   Served bean soup, parched wheat,
And late summer honey.

37   Seven tables, seven couches,
Poppy cakes, flaxseed cakes,
Sesame cakes, drinking cups
Of beaten gold.

38   There are three seasons:
Summer and winter,
And autumn is the third,
And spring is the fourth,
When everything flowers
And nobody has enough
To eat.

39   The valleys are asleep and the mountaintops,
The sea cliffs and the mountain streams,
Serpents and lizards born from the black earth,
The forest animals and beeswarms in their hives,
The fish in the salt deep of the violet sea.
And the long-winged birds.

40   Rhipa, mountain flowered with forests
Dark as night in their depths.

41   Artemis! O thou dressed
In wild animal skins.

42   Never shall these old legs dance again,
My honey-throated, high-singing girls!

Had I the wish, well wouldn't I be
The cock of the blue sea-bird
Who flies forever with his hens
Over the foam-flowered ocean waves?
O careless heart, sea-purple holy bird.

43   Short the way, but pitiless
The need to walk it.

44   Whoever they are,
Neighbors are neighbors.

45   A collar of gold
Studded with florets
Of rich red.

46   I can whistle
Every bird's song.

47   Boast and brag, such was his fame.
Love You All was his good wife's name.

48   Eating and singing and the soldiers
Nearby begin a hymn to Apollo.

49   Come dancing, come singing,
Bright-eyed angel of music,
Join us in song, in praise,
Master of the graceful foot,
O Kalliopa, daughter of Zeus.

50   This is the music Alkman made
From partridge dance and partridge song
With his flittering partridge tongue.

ANAKREON

1   Nor [   ] among
Your fellows be so fearful and timid,
My boy with the handsomest eyes.

Thinks you steadfast too [   ]
Plotting [   ]
Affectionately to beguile [   ]

In those blue fields of hyacinths,
Kypris unharnessing the horses,
Turned them loose untethered [   ]

[   ] and in the middle break
[   ] at which so many
Hearts of our fellows took fright.

You whore, Herotimé, you whore
[   ]
[   ].

2   Fists in trouble flying [   ]
[   ] I see your chin kept up
[   ] and owe you much [ ]
[   ] turning from love's grace
[   ] charmbound hand and foot
Through Aphrodite's entanglements
[   ] bring water and wine [   ]

[   ] summon [   ]
Grace [.   ].

3   [   ]
       [   ] all [nig]ht long [   ]
       [   ]
       Both delight and [   ]
       [   ]
       But loving [   ]
       Offerings at hand [   ]
       Of the Pierides [   ]
       [   ]
       And Graces [   ]
       And then the [   ]
       [   ]
       [   ]
       [   ] beaut[iful] [   ]
       [   ]
       Flitter we all the night [   ]
       Fishing with bait [   ]
       Golden-helmeted Pallas [   ]
       [   ] from afar [   ]
       Flowering [   ]
       [   ].

4   [   ]
       And your curls in lovely bunches
       All shadowy around your slender neck.

       You are now as close-cropped as a calf,
       And your hair in ravaged handfuls
       Lies scattered in heaps on the black ground.
       Poor hair! Laid waste by the snippers.
       What grief I suffer to see it there.
       And what can anybody do about it now?

5   [   ] take pity on
          The famous woman imploring her god
          In anguish so many times over.

          How much better off had I been
          If you had thrown me, mother,
          Into the tall bright waves
          Of the ungiving sea [   ].

6   O deerslayer Artemis,
          God's bright-haired daughter,
          Packmaster of animals
          In the mountain forests,
          I ask at your knees
          That you come where
          The Lethaios tumbles
          To keep guard over us
          In our city and be
          Shepherdess as well
          Of settled civil folk.

7   This is the man who faced down
          The black shields of the Ialysian guard.

8   Butlers in the infantry
          Are disasters in the bud.

9   That good-natured cadet Megistes
          For going on ten months now
          Has sported the willow garland
          And cadged our honied wine.

10   A revolt, O Megistes,
          Has toppled holy [Samos].

11   You'll have me the gossip
         all over the neighborhood.

12   The talents that tantalized
         Talented Tantalos [tantalize me].

13   Bring me the winebowl, come my boy,
         To drink in one long swallow back,
         Ten cups of water, five of wine,
         And do me proud before its god.
         [   ]
         And have done with all this drinking
         In loud and drunken Scythian ways.
         Drink well and sing fine songs. Drink well,
         Sing fine songs to the god of wine.

14   O lord playing with Eros the wrecker,
         With blue-eyed mountain girls,
         With Aphrodite robed in red
         Along the highest ridges of the hills,
         To you I go down on my knees.
         Come, I beg you, kindly to me,
         And make Kleoboulos willing, O Deunysos,
         When I tell him that I love him.

15   Here—*ha!*—is Eros blond as gold
         Throwing his red ball at my head
         To make me come outside and play
         With a charming girl in embroidered shoes
         Who is, as you might know of course,
         Both well born and from Lesbos too,
         And tells me that my hair is white,
         And says *oh!* she loves another.

16   I look with longing at,
             I love, I worship Kleoboulos.

17   Boy, because you do not know
             You hold the reins that guide my heart,
             My look so searching glances off
             Your eyes as pretty as a girl's.

18   I would not wish on
             Amalthiê's horn,
             Not for a life lasting
             A hundred and fifty years,
             Not to be King Arganthonios
             Ruling over Tartessos
             Where everybody's happy.

19   In the month of Posideion,
             When the clouds are fat with rain,
             Wild storms bring us Zeus.

20   Can myrrh rubbed on a chest
             Sweeten the great round heart inside?

21   Targelios marvels at the skill
             With which you hurl the discus.

22   And Deunysos shouting
             So much, so loud.

23   But O Smerdias
             Is three times friskier
             Than [   ]

24   Because you were
        Stubborn with me.

25   You turn in your tracks
        When Leukippê [passes by].

26   But he, high-minded,
        [   ].

27   Not my gentle sister.

28   I am neither steadfast with
        Nor kind to my fellow man.

29   Eurypylê the blonde
        Is smitten with the
        Litterborne Artemon.

30   I've eaten a piece of wheatmeal biscuit
        But drunk an amphora of wine,
        And now I play a handsome song
        On the lute for a handsome boy.

31   I play Lydian octaves
        On twenty strings,
        While you, O Leukaspis,
        Play the fool.

32   [   ]
        Whose heart is green and young again
        And dances to a lissome tune on the flute.

33   I climb the white cliff again
              To throw myself into the grey sea,
              Drunk with love again.

34   The Mysians first mated horsemounting asses
              With mares, inventing the halfass mule.

35   To Olympos on easy wings
              I got to complain that my boy
              Will not do boyish things with me.

36   [Eros] romps around
              My grey beard.
              His wings flash gold
              [   ]
              Hippokleides pays
              No attention at all.

37   O the light of your loving smiling friendly face!

38   To Hera will I take [   ]
              [   ]
              Throw his shield into the smooth water
              Of the river [   ].

39   [   ] loved pitiful war.

40   The servant girl poured
              Honied wine from the jug
              On her shoulder.

41   [   ] and way back when
The enticing godling Peitho's eyes
Did not shine so much like money.

42   I come from the river
With bright things in my arms.

43   There, with the beautiful lyre,
That's Simalos in the choir.

44   I asked Strattis the maker of lyres
To let his hair grow out long.

45   Time was, he wore a tunic from a rummage sale,
A barbarian kind of hat, knucklebones in his ears,
And a cloak that used to be a rawhide shieldcase,
Artemon the pimp who got rich selling the use
Of bakers' apprentices and teenaged nancy boys,
Often seen in the stocks by his neck, or on the wheel,
Or having the lash applied to his bleeding back,
Or his beard and the hair on his head pulled out,
And now he rides in a mule cart, wears golden earrings,
Says he's the son of Kylê, and carries an ivory parasol
Like the women [   ].

46   You are kind to strangers, are you not?
I am thirsty. Let me drink.

47   They danced nimbly,
The beautiful-haired
Daughters of God.

48   Now the walls crowning the city
              Are destroyed [   ].

49   [He was] neither
              From our country
              Nor handsome.

50   Ares the raiser of dust
              Loves an unyielding fighter.

51   Sweetly singing
              Swiftly swerving
              Swallow.

52   Baldheaded Alexis
              Is courting another wife.

53   And now my hair is thin and white,
              Grizzled the locks above my ears.
              Youth's gone, and with it, all delight.
              My teeth are going with the years.

              What time remains is short and sweet.
              Therefore I often cry and dread
              Dark Tartaros where I shall meet
              In dreary rooms the weeping dead.

              For Hades' house is dark, and black
              The downward road, the hateful way,
              Unwilling and with no way back,
              Downward ever, and there to stay.

54   Bring water and bring wine
        And garlands of honeysuckle
        And yourself alone, my bonny boy.
        I must wrestle Eros down.

55   They wore plaited garlands
        Of clover across their chests.

56   Toss knucklebones with Eros:
        Madness and confusion every throw.

57   Took off her dress
        And went naked
        Like a Dorian.

58   Off to Pythomandros',
        Trying to elude Eros.

59   I take up my shield.
        The strap is of Karian make.

60   I love it when we play together.
        You do it with such grace and verve.

61   Here is Eros. If he remains,
        Beauty will have to do for brains.

62   Boys will love me still
        When I am gone.
        In their ears my tongue
        Will yet trill on.

My words, my music
Will survive
And be loved as I would be
Were I alive.

63   I slide by, but as over
Rocks hidden in the sea.

64   Young and healthy.

65   As wretched as if dead.

66   Made off with much treasure.

67   And then be gracious with,
O loving friend, your slender thighs.

68   Be as gentle with that boy as with a suckling fawn
Lost in the forest from its antlered mother.

69   Into a clean jug pour
The wine mixed five to three.

70   Garlands of celery around our brows,
We're off to celebrate the Dionysia.

71   Let me die. No other way
Can I be free of this grief.

72   The wide-legged dance
Of Dionysos' Bassarids.

73   Show me the way to go home.
I'm drunk and I need to go to bed.

74   Eros the blacksmith
Hammers me again,
Striking while I'm hot,
And thrusts me sizzling
In the ice-cold stream.

75   You've snipped the delicious blossoms off,
Your perfect curls [with your own hand].

76   [   ] has an elbow
For Sicilian dice.

77   I despise the rude, earthy manners
Of these barbarians. But you,
Megistês, are as shy as a child.

78   Watch me out of the corners of your eyes,
Do you, Thracian colt? Prance away, do you,
As if I didn't know how to catch you?
You'd better know that I can bridle you,
Rein you in, ride you to the finish line.
You play in the meadow, nibbling, romping.
That's for now. Soon enough I'll break you in.

79   Girl in a golden robe,
Girl with curly hair,

Listen to an old man,
Listen to me.

80   Of all my stalwart friends, Aristokleides,
            I grieve most for you, who died young
            To keep your country free.

81   When my dark hair
            Shall be streaked with white.

82   The edge of my spirit dulled.

83   Shaking your Thracian mane.

84   Silence, O God,
            Those who speak
            Such awful Greek.

85   [   ] bedroom
            In which he, unmarrying,
            Was married [   ].

86   As comfortable as travelers who ask only
            To come in out of the cold and sit by the fire.

87   Once, long ago,
            the Milesians were brave.

88   Quit chattering on
            Like the waves of the sea

To the accompaniment
Of Gastrodora's laughter
Clanging like bronze,
Both of you drinking
From the winejar by the fire.

89 I am perhaps in love
Again, perhaps not,
And crazy to boot.
No, not crazy.

90 Let him who wants
To fight fight.

91 You carry on over it
Far too much.

92 He sleeps soundly
With his bedroom door
Always unbolted.

93 I become misty-eyed and ready
When you want me.

94 And I, I took the cup
And drained it in honor
To the whitemaned Erxion.

95 Men each wearing three garlands,
Two of roses and one of marjoram.

96   [Tables] sagging with their load
                 Of good things [to eat].

97   Plunging our hands into the stewpot.

98   Like the cuckoo,
                 I made myself scarce
                 When she was about.

99   [   ] wants
                 To seduce us.

100   Twining thigh with thigh.

101   Lovely, too lovely,
                 And too many love you.

102   Cut the collar through
                 [   ]
                 Ripped the coat down the back.

103   As drunk and rolling
                 As if he were Dionysos.

104   [Spring wind] shakes
                 The darkleaved laurel and green olive tree.

105   [   ]
                 Glowing with desire,

Gleaming with spiced oil
[   ].

106   [Eros'] wanton, reckless, aimless
Arrows circle around my ears.

107   Sea-purple dye.

108   [The beauty of water,]
The dwelling of nymphs.

109   [Kallikritê, Kyanê's daughter]
Rules as a tyrant.

110   Drinking Eros.

111   The sun beautifully bright.

112   Walking along with a haughty neck.

113   Chattering swallow.

114   Wine-server.

115   Wine-drinking woman.

116   Swift colts.

117   A filthy behind.

118   Walking with swaying hips.

119   When the winejar goes around,
               Silence the man whose gossip's war,
               Grief of fighting, ugly death.
               With wine we want the talk to be
               Of Aphrodite's glancing eye
               And supple dancers to the lyre.

120   Eros melting in the mouth.

121   INSCRIPTION ON A HERM
               Pray to Hermes, friend and stranger,
               For Timonax who put me here
               Splendid before these lovely doors
               To honor the messenger of the gods.
               Welcome to my gymnasium, all.

122   Eros heavy on my shoulders.

123   Pretty.

124   Stalks of slim white celery
               In a wicker basket.

125   (A mare named Breeze belonging to Pheidolas the Corinthian
               threw her jockey soon after the field left the gate on the track at
               Elis. She raced on, however, just as if she had a mount, turned

at the post, improved her gallop as she heard the trumpet,
crossed the finish line first, and stopped, seeing that she had won.
The umpires announced Pheidolas the winner and gave him
permission to set up a statue of Breeze at Olympia.
    — Pausanias, *Travels in Greece: Elis II* [Book VI:13].)

This is Pheidolas' mare, name of Breeze,
Raised in Korinthos of the double dancing floors,
Standing here, honor to Kronos' son, that we remember
The splendor of her legs.

126   [Teos] the daughter of Athamas.

127   Aithiopian child.

128   Short straight [Persian] sword.

129   To rise up [lightly and swiftly
    As an arrow of elder wood].

130   He was a soldier in the wars.
    Timokritos. This is his grave.
    Sometimes unkind Ares kills
    Not the cowards but the brave.

131   Sauce.

132   Stubborn [as a mule].

133   Side saddle.

134   For Zeus Prexidikê sewed
                 This cloak Dyseris designed.
                 Two arts, one mind.

135   Self-admiring.

136   The flute of handsome Bathyllos.

137   [Crowned with garlands of myrtle,
                 Coriander, willow, marjoram, aniseed].

138   Knockkneed [coward].

139   Mother of two children.

140   Brave Agathon died for Abdera.
                 All Abdera wept at his pyre.
                 The blooddrinker Ares had never
                 Met such a fire as his fire.

141   He understood.

142   He gave pleasure.

143   Affectionately [drunk].

144   INSCRIPTION ON AN ALTARPIECE
                 Elikonias carries the thyrsos

Between Xanthippê and Glaukê,
Dancing down from the mountain,
Bringing with them grapes, ivy,
And a goat [for Dionysos].

145   In a sacred manner.

146   The kalyx of a flower.

147   Worthy of being spit on.

148   INSCRIPTION ON A HERM
I was put here first by Kallitelês
Whose children have put me here again,
A new image. Stand, all, and pray.

149   Lydianized gentry.

150   To gaze in fear.

151   Polykrates.

152   To cry in grief.

153   A song of praise.

154   Phillos.

155   Graceful.

156   As white as milk.

157   Prouder of his sword than Peleus.

158   [   ]

159   I am the shield which brought Python home alive.
                 Now I hang in Athena's quiet sanctuary, her gift.

160   Grace to the son of Aiskhylos, Silver Bow.
                 Give thanks, Apollo, to worshipping Naukrates.

161   [   ]
                 Again [   ] island
                 [   ] we two in love,
                 We pray *O ears that hear prayers,*
                 Our very solemn [   ]
                 [   ] Lady in the stars
                 [   ] Eros stalking
                 On the balls of his feet [   ]
                 The happy [   ] who
                 Of those I love [   ]
                 Until my dream [   ]
                 Hail! Kyllanas [   ]
                 [   ] the sea [   ]
                 We kneel at Aphrodite's altar
                 [   ]
                 Sacred mother [   ]
                 Of Kypris [   ]
                 [   ]

Excite [   ]
[   ]
Glossy [   ]
[   ]
Sweet [   ]
Hail [   ]
Sight [   ]
I hug your knees [   ]
Young [   ]
You, boy [   ]
Come to me! [   ]
Look [   ]
[   ].

162   *A line of Anakreon coming from the mouth of*
            Ekphantides in a vase drawing by Euphronios:

O Apollon, and you, Ho[ly Artemis!]

HERAKLEITOS

1   The Logos is eternal
but men have not heard it
and men have heard it and not understood.

Through the Logos all things are understood
yet men do not understand
as you shall see when you put acts and words to the test
I am going to propose:

One must talk about everything according to its nature,
how it comes to be and how it grows.
Men have talked about the world without paying attention
to the world or to their own minds,
as if they were asleep or absent-minded.

2   Let us therefore notice that understanding is common to all
men. Understanding is common to all, yet each man acts as if
his intelligence were private and all his own.

3   Men who wish to know about the world must learn about it
in its particular details.

4   Men dig up and search through much earth to find gold.

5   Our understanding of the greatest matters will never be
complete.

6   Knowledge is not intelligence.

7   I have heard many men talk, but none who realized that understanding is distinct from all other knowledge.

8   I have looked diligently at my own mind.

9   It is natural for man to know his own mind and to be sane.

10   Sanity is the highest excellence. The skillful mind speaks the truth, knowing how everything is separate in its own being.

11   I honor what can be seen, what can be heard, what can be learned.

12   Eyes are better informers than ears.

13   Eyes and ears are poor informers to the barbarian mind.

14   One ought not to talk or act as if he were asleep.

15   We share a world when we are awake; each sleeper is in a world of his own.

16   Awake, we see a dying world; asleep, dreams.

17   Nature loves to hide. [Becoming is a secret process].

18   The Lord who prophesies at Delphoi neither speaks clearly nor hides his meaning completely; he gives one symbols instead.

19   In searching out the truth be ready for the unexpected, for it is difficult to find and puzzling when you find it.

20   Everything flows; nothing remains. [Everything moves; nothing is still. Everything passes away; nothing lasts.]

21   One cannot step twice into the same river, for the water into which you first stepped has flowed on.

22   Cold things become hot; hot things, cold. Wet things, dry; dry things, wet.

23   Change alone is unchanging.

24   History is a child building a sand-castle by the sea, and that child is the whole majesty of man's power in the world.

25   War is the father of us all and our king. War discloses who is godlike and who is but a man, who is a slave and who is freeman.

26   It must be seen clearly that war is the natural state of man. Justice is contention. Through contention all things come to be.

27   When Homer said that he wished war might disappear from the lives of gods and men, he forgot that without opposition all things would cease to exist.

28   Everything becomes fire, and from fire everything is born, as in the eternal exchange of money and merchandise.

29   This world, which is always the same for all men, neither god nor man made: it has always been, it is, and always shall be: an everlasting fire rhythmically dying and flaring up again.

30   Not enough and too much.

31   Divides and rejoins, goes forward and then backward.

32   The first metamorphosis of fire is to become the sea, and half of the sea becomes the earth, half the flash of lightning.

33   As much earth is washed into the sea as sea-stuff dries and becomes part of the shore.

34   The life of fire comes from the death of earth. The life of air comes from the death of fire. The life of water comes from the death of air. The life of earth comes from the death of water.

35   Lightning is the lord of everything.

36   There is a new sun for every day.

37   The sun is one foot wide.

38   If there were no sun, all the other stars together could not dispell the night.

39   Morning is distinguished from evening by the Bear who rises and sets diametrically across from the path of Zeus of the Burning Air.

40   The most beautiful order of the world is still a random gathering of things insignificant in themselves.

41   All beasts are driven to pasture.

42   No matter how many ways you try, you cannot find a boundary to consciousness, so deep in every direction does it extend.

43   The stuff of the psyche is a smoke-like substance of finest particles that gives rise to all other things; its particles are of less mass than any other substance and it is constantly in motion: only movement can know movement.

44   The psyche rises as a mist from things that are wet.

45   The psyche grows according to its own law.

46   A dry psyche is most skilled in intelligence and is brightest in virtue.

47   The psyche lusts to be wet [and to die].

48   A drunk man, staggering and mindless, must be led home by his son, so wet is his psyche.

49   Water brings death to the psyche, as earth brings death to water. Yet water is born of earth, and the psyche from water.

50   That delicious drink, spiced hot Pramnian wine mixed with resin, roasted barley, and grated goat's cheese, separates in the bowl if it is not stirred.

51   It is hard to withstand the heart's desire, and it gets what it wants at the psyche's expense.

52   If every man had exactly what he wanted, he would be no better than he is now.

53   Hide our ignorance as we will, an evening of wine reveals it.

54   The untrained mind shivers with excitement at everything it hears.

55   The stupid are deaf to truth: they hear, but think that the wisdom of a perception always applies to someone else.

56   Bigotry is the disease of the religious.

57   Many people learn nothing from what they see and experience, nor do they understand what they hear explained, but imagine that they have.

58   If everything were smoke, all perception would be by smell.

59   In Hades psyches perceive each other by smell alone.

60   The dead body is useless even as manure.

61   Men are not intelligent, the gods are intelligent.

62   The mind of man exists in a logical universe but is not itself logical.

63   The gods' presence in the world goes unnoticed by men who do not believe in the gods.

64   Man, who is an organic continuation of the Logos, thinks he can sever that continuity and exist apart from it.

65   At night we extinguish the lamp and go to sleep; at death our lamp is extinguished and we go to sleep.

66   Gods become men; men become gods, the one living the death of the other, the other dying the life of the one.

[*Wheelwright translates:* Immortals become mortals, mortals become immortals; they live in each other's death and die in each other's life.]

67   In death men will come upon things they do not expect, things utterly unknown to the living.

68   We assume a new being in death: we become protectors of the living and the dead.

69   Character is fate.

70   The greater the stakes, the greater the loss. [The more one puts oneself at the mercy of chance, the more chance will involve one in the laws of necessity and inevitability.]

71   Justice stalks the liar and the false witness.

72   Fire catches up with everything, in time.

73   How can you hide from what never goes away?

74   There are gods here, too.

75   They pray to statues of gods and heroes much as they would gossip with the wall of a house, understanding so little of gods and heroes.

76   Paraders by night, magicians, Bacchantes, leapers to the
flute and drum, initiates in the Mysteries—what men call
the Mysteries are unholy disturbances of the peace.

77   Their pompous hymns and phallic songs would be obscene
if we did not understand that they are the rites of Dionysos.
And Dionysos, through whom they go into a trance and
speak in tongues and for whom they beat the drum, do they
realize that he is the same god as Hades, Lord of the Dead?

78   They cleanse themselves with blood: as if a man fallen into
the pigsty should wash himself with slop. To one who does
not know what's happening, the religious man at his rites
seems to be a man who has lost his mind.

79   There is madness in the Sibyl's voice, her words are
gloomy, ugly, and rough, but they are true for a thousand
years, because a god speaks through her.

80   All men think.

81   All men should speak clearly and logically, and thus share
rational discourse and have a body of thought in common,
as the people of a city are all under the same laws. The laws
of men derive from the divine law, which is whole and
single, which penetrates as it will to satisfy human pur-
poses, but is mightier than any law known to men.

82   Defend the law as you would the city wall.

83   Law gives the people a single will to obey.

84   One man, to my way of thinking, is worth ten thousand, if he's the best of his kind.

85   The best of men see only one thing worth having: undying fame. They prefer fame to wealth. The majority of men graze like cattle.

86   Those killed by Ares are honored by gods and men.

87   The man of greatest reputation knows how to defend a reputation.

88   Extinguish pride as quickly as you would a fire.

89   To do the same thing over and over is not only boredom: it is to be controlled by rather than to control what you do.

90   Dogs bark at strangers.

91   What do they have for intellect, for common sense, who believe the myths of public singers and flock with the crowd as if public opinion were a teacher, forgetting that the many are bad, the few are good [there are many bad people, few good ones]?

92   All men are equally mystified by unaccountable evidence, even Homer, wisest of the Greeks. He was mystified by children catching lice. He heard them say, What we have found and caught we throw away; what we have not found and caught we still have.

93   Homer should be thrown out of the games and whipped,
           and Archilochos with him.

94   Good days and bad days, says Hesiod, forgetting that all
           days are alike.

95   The Ephesians might as well all hang themselves and let
           the city be governed by children. They have banished
           Hermadoros, best of their citizens, because they cannot
           abide to have among them a man so much better than
           they are.

96   Ephesians, be rich! I cannot wish you worse.

97   Life is bitter and fatal, yet men cherish it and beget chil-
           dren to suffer the same fate.

98   Opposites cooperate. The beautifullest harmonies come
           from opposition. All things repel each other.

99   We know health by illness, good by evil, satisfaction by
           hunger, leisure by fatigue.

100   Except for what things would we never have heard the
           word justice?

101   Sea water is both fresh and foul: excellent for fish, poison
           to men.

102   Asses would rather have hay than gold.

103   Pigs wash in mud, chickens in dust.

104   The handsomest ape is uglier than the ugliest man. The wisest man is less wise, less beautiful than a god: the distance from ape to man is that from man to god.

105   A boy is to a man as a man is to a god.

106   To God all is beautiful, good, and as it should be. Man must see things as either good or bad.

107   Having cut, burned and poisoned the sick, the doctor then submits his bill.

108   The same road goes both up and down.

109   The beginning of a circle is also its end.

110   The river we stepped into is not the river in which we stand.

111   Curled wool, straight thread.

112   Joints are and are not parts of the body. They cooperate through opposition, and make a harmony of separate forces. Wholeness arises from distinct particulars; distinct particulars occur in wholeness.

113   To live is to die, to be awake is to sleep, to be young is to
be old, for the one flows into the other, and the process is
capable of being reversed.

114   Hesiod, so wise a teacher, did not see that night and day
are the same.

115   A bow is alive only when it kills.

116   The unseen design of things is more harmonious than the
seen.

117   We do not notice how opposing forces agree. Look at the
bow and the lyre.

118   Not I but the world says it: All is one.

119   Wisdom alone is whole, and is both willing and unwilling
to be named Zeus.

120   Wisdom is whole: the knowledge of how things are plot-
ted in their courses by all other things.

121   God is day night winter summer war peace enough too
little, but disguised in each and known in each by a sepa-
rate flavor.

122   The sun will never change the rhythm of its motion. If it
did, the Erinyes, agents of justice, would bring it to trial.

123   All things come in seasons.

124   Even sleeping men are doing the world's business and helping it along.

DIOGENES

1   I have come to debase the coinage.

2   All things belong to the gods. Friends own things in common. Good men are friends of the gods. All things belong to the good.

3   Men nowhere, but real boys at Sparta.

4   I am a yapping Maltese lap dog when hungry, a Molossian wolfhound when fed, breeds tedious to hunt with but useful for guarding the house and the sheepfold.

5   No one can live with me as a companion: it would be too inconvenient.

6   It is absurd to bring back a runaway slave. If a slave can survive without a master, is it not awful to admit that the master cannot live without the slave?

7   I am a citizen of the world.

8   We are not as hardy, free, or accomplished as animals.

9   If only I could free myself from hunger as easily as from desire.

10   Of what use is a philosopher who doesn't hurt anybody's feelings?

11   Demosthenes is a Scythian in his speeches and a gentleman on the battlefield.

12   The darkest place in the tavern is the most conspicuous.

13   I am Athens' one free man.

14   The porches and streets of Athens were built for me as a place to live.

15   I learned from the mice how to get along: no rent, no taxes, no grocery bill.

16   Plato winces when I track dust across his rugs: he knows that I'm walking on his vanity.

17   How proud you are of not being proud, Plato says, and I reply that there is pride and pride.

18   When I die, throw me to the wolves. I'm used to it.

19   A man keeps and feeds a lion. The lion owns a man.

20   The art of being a slave is to rule one's master.

21   Everything is of one substance. It is custom, not reason, that sets the temple apart from the house, mutton from human flesh for the table, bread from vegetable, vegetable from meat.

22   Antisthenes made me an exiled beggar dressed in rags: wise, independent, and content.

23   It is luckier to be a Megarian's ram than his son.

24   Before begging it is useful to practice on statues.

25   When the Sinopians ostracized me from Pontos, they condemned themselves to a life without me.

26   Aristotle dines at King Philip's convenience, Diogenes at his own.

27   When Plato said that if I'd gone to the Sicilian court as I was invited, I wouldn't have to wash lettuce for a living, I replied that if he washed lettuce for a living he wouldn't have had to go to the Sicilian court.

28   Philosophy can turn a young man from the love of a beautiful body to the love of a beautiful mind.

29   When I was captured behind the Macedonian lines and taken before Philip as a spy, I said that I'd only come to see how big a fool a king can be.

30   A. I am Alexander the Great.
          B. I am Diogenes, the dog.
          A. The dog?
          B. I nuzzle the kind, bark at the greedy, and bite louts.
          A. What can I do for you?
          B. Stand out of my light.

31   To live is not itself an evil, as has been claimed, but to lead a worthless life is.

32   They laugh at me, but I'm not laughed at.

33   Great crowds at the Olympic games, but not of people.

34   The Shahinshah of Persia moves in pomp from Susa in the spring, from Babylon in the winter, from Media in the summer, and Diogenes walks every year from Athens to Corinth, and back again from Corinth to Athens.

35   I threw my cup away when I saw a child drinking from his hands at the trough.

36   Go into any whorehouse and learn the worthlessness of the expensive.

37   We can only explain you, young man, by assuming that your father was drunk the night he begot you.

38   Can you believe that Pataikion the thief will fare better in Elysion because of his initiation into the Mysteries than Epameinondas the Pythagorean?

39   One wrong will not balance another: to be honorable and just is our only defense against men without honor or justice.

40   To be saved from folly you need either kind friends or fierce enemies.

41   Watching a mouse can cure you of jealousy of others' good fortune.

42   There is no stick hard enough to drive me away from a man from whom I can learn something.

43   Eukleidos' lectures limp and sprawl, Plato's are tedious, tragedies are quarrels before an audience, and politicians are magnified butlers.

44   Watch a doctor, philosopher, or helmsman, and you will conclude that man is the most intelligent of the animals, but then, regard the psychiatrist and the astrologer and their clients, and those who think they are superior because they are rich. Can creation display a greater fool than man?

45   Reason or a halter.

46   Why Syrakousa, friend Plato? Are not the olives in Attika just as toothsome?

47   Plato's philosophy is an endless conversation.

48   Beg a cup of wine from Plato and he will send you a whole
jar. He does not give as he is asked, nor answer as he is
questioned.

49   Share a dish of dried figs with Plato and he will take them
all.

50   Grammarians without any character at all lecture us on
that of Odysseus.

51   The contest that should be for truth and virtue is for sway
and belongings instead.

52   Happy the man who thinks to marry and changes his mind,
who plans a voyage he does not take, who runs for office
but withdraws his name, who wants to belong to the circle
of an influential man, but is excluded.

53   A friend's hand is open.

54   Bury me prone: I have always faced the other way.

55   Raising sons: teach them poetry, history, and philosophy.
Geometry and music are not essential, and can be learned
later. Teach them to ride a horse, to shoot a true bow, to
master the slingshot and javelin. At the gymnasium they
should exercise only so much as gives them a good color
and a trim body. Teach them to wait upon themselves at
home, and to enjoy ordinary food, and to drink water rather
than wine. Crop their hair close. No ornaments. Have

them wear a thin smock, go barefoot, be silent, and never gawk at people on the street.

56   In the rich man's house there is no place to spit but in his face.

57   The luxurious have made frugality an affliction.

58   I'm turning that invitation down: the last time I was there, they were not thankful enough that I came.

59   When some strangers to Athens asked me to show them Demosthenes, I gave them the finger, so that they would know what it felt like to meet him.

60   A choirmaster pitches the note higher than he knows the choristers can manage. So do I.

61   Go about with your middle finger up and people will say you're daft; go about with your little finger out, and they will cultivate your acquaintance.

62   For three thousand drachmas you can get a statue, for two coppers a quart of barley.

63   Masters should obey their slaves; patients, their doctors; rivers, their banks.

64   Against fate I put courage; against custom, nature; against passion, reason.

65   Toadying extends even to Diogenes, I say to the mice who nibble my crumbs.

66   Even with a lamp in broad daylight I cannot find an honest man.

67   There are gods. How else explain people like Lysias the apothecary on whom the gods have so obviously turned their backs?

68   You can no more improve yourself by sacrificing at the altar than you can correct your grammar.

69   We are more curious about the meaning of dreams than about things we see when awake.

70   Pilfering Treasury property is particularly dangerous: big thieves are ruthless in punishing little thieves.

71   It is not for charity but my salary that I beg in the streets.

72   Had to lift its skirt to see whether man or woman had stopped me to talk philosophy.

73   I pissed on the man who called me a dog. Why was he so surprised?

74   Pitching heeltaps: the better you are at it, the worse for you.

75   You know the kind of luckless folk we call triple wretches.
             Well, these professors and others of that kidney who long
             to be known as famous lecturers are triple Greeks.

76   The ignorant rich, sheep with golden fleeces.

77   The athlete's brain, like his body, is as strong as that of a
             bull.

78   Love of money is the marketplace for every evil.

79   A good man is a picture of a god.

80   Running errands for Eros is the business of the idle.

81   The greatest misery is to be old, poor, and alone.

82   The deadliest bite among wild animals is that of the boot-
             licker; amongst tame, that of the flatterer.

83   Choked on the honey of flattery.

84   The stomach is our life's Charybdis.

85   The golden Aphrodite that Phryne put up at Delphoi
             should be inscribed *Greek Lechery, Its Monument.*

86   A pretty whore is poisoned honey.

87   If, as they say, I am only an ignorant man trying to be a philosopher, then that may be what a philosopher is.

88   People who talk well but do nothing are like musical instruments: the sound is all they have to offer.

89   Aren't you ashamed, I said to the prissy young man, to assume a lower rank in nature than you were given?

90   Be careful that your pomade doesn't cause the rest of you to stink.

91   Why do we call house slaves footmen? Well, it's because they are men and they have feet.

92   What lovers really enjoy are their spats and the disapproval of society.

93   Beggars get handouts before philosophers because people have some idea of what it's like to be blind and lame.

94   If your cloak was a gift, I appreciate it; if it was a loan, I'm not through with it yet.

95   Why praise Diokles for giving me a drachma and not me for deserving it?

96   I have seen the victor Dioxippos subdue all contenders at Olympia and be thrown on his back by the glance of a girl.

97   To own nothing is the beginning of happiness.

98   Every day's a festival to the upright.

99   Why not whip the teacher when the pupil misbehaves?

100   I had my lunch in the courtroom because that's where I was hungry.

101   It is a convenience not to fear the dark.

102   Discourse on virtue and they pass by in droves, whistle and dance the shimmy, and you've got an audience.

103   After grace and a prayer for health, the banqueters set to and eat themselves into an apoplexy.

104   To a woman who had flopped down before an altar with her butt in the air I remarked in passing that the god was also behind her.

105   At Khrysippos' lecture I saw the blank space coming up on the scroll, and said to the audience: Cheer up, fellows, land is in sight!

106   We have complicated every simple gift of the gods.

107   Make passes at you, do they? Why, then, don't you wear clothes that don't so accurately outline what they're interested in?

108   After a visit to the baths, where do you go to have a wash?

109   I've seen Plato's cups and table, but not his cupness and tableness.

110   If you've turned yourself out so handsomely, young man, for men, it's unfortunate; if for women, it's unfair.

111   A blush is the color of virtue.

112   A lecher is a fig tree on a cliff: crows get the figs.

113   The road from Sparta to Athens is like the passageway in a house from the men's rooms to the women's.

114   An obol now, friend, and when the community asks you to contribute for my funeral, you can say that you've already given.

115   I was once as young and silly as you are now, but I doubt if you will become as old and wise as I am.

116   Begging from fat Anaximenes, I argued what an advantage it would be to him to share the makings of that paunch with the poor.

117   There is no society without law, no civilization without a city.

118   The only real commonwealth is the whole world.

119 Practice makes perfect.

120 Learn the pleasure of despising pleasure.

121 Education disciplines the young, comforts the old, is the wealth of the poor, and civilizes the rich.

122 The greatest beauty of human kind is frankness.

123 Plato begs too, but like Telemakhos conversing with Athena, with lowered head, so that others may not over-hear.

124 Give up philosophy because I'm an old man? It's at the end of a race that you break into a burst of speed.

HERONDAS

I. The Matchmaker

(*The actor sets out his traps while his boy beats a jangling tambourine which, as an audience gathers, gives way to a sprightly jig on a flute. The actor places two stools and opens his box of props and costumes. He dons a dress, a wig, a stole. His eyes are made up female. He trots primly, with swaying hips, to one of the stools, giving a glad eye to the audience on the way. He settles himself, arranges the stole with pompous dignity, bats his eyes, purses his lips, consults an imaginary hand mirror, and becomes an important matron serenely at home. She holds this pose until the boy raps on the box, whereupon her composure is shattered and she yelps on a high note.*)

METRIKHÉ
Threissa! Somebody's knocking at the front.
Go see if it's not a country peddler
Selling door to door.

(*Actor tosses his stole and wig to the boy, deftly catching a wig of younger, girlish hair, and an apron. He springs to the imaginary door, wiping his hands on the apron, looking dumb and scared. His accent becomes lower class and Thracian. He talks through the closed door.*)

THREISSA
                    Who's there at the door?

(*He ventriloquizes the answer.*)

GYLLIS
It's me who's here!

THREISSA
                    Who's me? You're afraid
To come on in, aren't you?

(*Horrified by the way she has put the question, covers her mouth with
both hands.*)

GYLLIS
                              I'm as in
As I can get till you open the door.

THREISSA
Yes, but who are you?

GYLLIS
                    It's Gyllis is who.
Philainion's mother. Tell Metrikhé
I've come to pay her sweet self a visit.

(*Switches wigs, stole for apron.*)

METRIKHÉ
Who is it, pray, at the door?

GYLLIS
                          It's Gyllis!
Mother Gyllis as ever was!

METRIKHÉ
                    Gyllis!

(*To Threissa, with shooing hands.*)

Make yourself scarce, slave. Off with you now, scat.
Gyllis! What stroke of good luck brings you by?
Like a god dropping down on us mortals!

It has been months, five or six, I'll swear,
Since I've had so much as a glimpse of you,
Not even in a dream. And here you are.

(*Jumps into the empty space to which she was talking, catching a tackier
stole and an old woman's out-of-date bonnet on the way. Stoops at the
shoulders, sucks in mouth, draws in on himself, losing height. Voice shaky
but chirpy.*)

GYLLIS
I don't live near, child, and as for the road
You can sink into the mud past your knees.
I'm as weak as a housefly, anyway.
I'm old, girl. Old age is my shadow now.

METRIKHÉ
Such talk. Exaggeration, all of it.
You wouldn't turn down a nudge, you know it.

GYLLIS

(*Cackles.*)

Make fun! You young women think we're all
Just like you.

METRIKHÉ

(*Pats hair, rolls eyes.*)

                    Well, don't include me, I'm sure!

GYLLIS
What I've come to see you about, my chit,
Is a word to the wise.

                    (*Grins horribly.*)

                    For how long now
Have you been deprived of a husband, dear?
How long alone in your bed? In Egypt,

On a business trip, is he, your Mandris?
It's five months he has been away and not
A letter of the alphabet from him.

(*Lets this sink in.*)

Hasn't he found another cup to sip?
Hasn't he forgotten you, don't you think?

(*Wide-eyed.*)

What I've heard of Egypt! Her very home,
The Goddess.

            (*Pats her groin.*)

                They've got everything there is,
Everything that grows, everything that's made.
Rich families, gymnasiums, money,
Peace, famous places and philosophers,
Grand sights, army, charming boys, the altar
Of their god who married his own sister.
They have a good king.

                (*Thinks hard for more.*)

                A museum. Wine.
Every wonderful thing you might want!
Also, by Koré the bride of Hades,
More women than there are stars in the sky,
And every one of them, dear Metrikhé,
As pretty as the lady goddesses
Who stood naked before Paris that time
To be sized up, forgive the expression.
God forbid they hear me put it like that.

(*Averts bad luck with a pious gesture.*)

Whatever then can you be thinking of,
My poor girl, to sit here doing nothing?
Bird on an empty nest! All fires go out,
Leaving ashes. Old age is for certain.
Perk up, look about, have a little fun.

Does a ship have only the one anchor?
It has two! When you're dead, you're dead.
Why should this one life be grey and dreary?

(*Quietly, reflectively.*)

It's uncertain enough for us women.

(*Brightens.*)

Perhaps you have somebody on the sly?

METRIKHÉ
Of course not!

GYLLIS
          Then listen well to me, dear.
I've come here with a jolly little plan.
There is a nice young man, name of Gryllos,
Pataikos' daughter Mataliné's son.
Five prizes in athletics has he won.
One in the Pythian Games at Delphi
When he was a mere stripling of a boy,
Two at Korinthos, the down on his cheeks,
Two at the Olympics, men's boxing match.

(*Warms to her subject.*)

And he is very well to do, sweetheart.
What's more, he has never mashed the grass down
In that way.

         (*Proud of her delicacy.*)

          That is, he is a virgin.
He has yet to press his seal in the wax.
He is still a stranger to Kythera.

(*Huddling closer.*)

And Metrikhé, he has fallen for you!
At the festival parade of Misa.
He is turned around, his insides stirred up.

Knowing my skill as a good matchmaker,
He came to me, tears in his handsome eyes,
Pestered me day and night, pitifully,
Near death, and said that love has laid him low.

(*Throws her arms wide, and stands hovering.*)

Metrikhé, poppet, give Aphrodite
Half a chance, one lovely sweet naughty fling.
We get old, all of us, quite soon enough.
You stand to gain two ways: you'll be loved,
And the boy is both rich and generous.
Look here, think what I am doing for you
And I'm doing it because I love you.

METRIKHÉ

(*Sternly, after a longish, shocked silence with downcast eyes.*)

You're as blind, Gyllis, as your hair's white.
By Demeter! By my faith in Mandris,
I would not so calmly have abided
Such cheek as this from anybody but you,
And that only because of your years.
I would have given such limping twaddle
Good reason to be lame. Better reason,
Still, to keep away from my door. Make sure,
Old woman, that you don't come here again
With rigmarole not fit for decent ears.
And do let me *sit here doing nothing*,
As you put it. Nobody gets away
With insulting my Mandris to my face.
Not what you came to hear, is it, Gyllis?

(*Expels breath in exasperation. Softens manner. Calls over shoulder.*)

Threissa! Wipe the black cup clean with a cloth,
Pour a tot in a dribble of water.
Bring Gyllis a little nip for the road.
There, Gyllis, drink up.

GYLLIS

(*Hurt.*)

                              Thank you, dear, but no.

(*Broods with pouting lip.*)

Metrikhé, sweet.

                    (*No reply.*)

                    I'm not here to tempt you.
I'm here on Lady Aphrodite's work.
It was at the festival he found love.
So religious.

METRIKHÉ

(*Throws up hands.*)

          On Aprhodite's work!

GYLLIS

(*Primly.*)

Yes.

METRIKHÉ

   Your health. Drink up. So nice you could come.

GYLLIS

(*Philosophically.*)

Lovely wine you have, dear. By Demeter.

(*Smacks lips.*)

Gyllis has never had any better.

(*Drains cup, with a lick around the rim.*)

I suppose now I'd best be on my way.
Sincerely yours, sweetheart. Keep well, and all.

(*Seeming to change the subject.*)

Myrtle and Tippy, they keep themselves young.
And myself, I can still shuffle around.

(*Actor shuffles, wags his behind, winks broadly, and takes his bow.*)

II. The Whorehouse Manager

(*Battaros, a whorehouse manager, is pleading a case of assault and battery against one Thales, captain of a merchant ship, in a law court in Kos. The actor wears a preposterously big Scythian moustache, a black roachy wig reeking of some fruity essence sharpened by pine oil. His eyes are raccooned with violet circles, his fingers are crowded with trashy rings, his robe is decidedly the color and cut for a dinner party but not for a court of law. He speaks with the brass and vulnerable dignity of an alley lawyer. His accent is foreign, with a trace of a lisp.*)

BATTAROS

(*In a pitched voice, with gestures.*)

Gentlemen of the court, it is not whom
We are, or the prestige we have downtown,
Nor whether Thales here owns a ship which
It is worth one hundred fifty thousand,
Or, as is true, I don't have bread to eat,
But whether he's going to do me dirt
Without he answers to the law for it.

(*Gasps, worn out by such eloquence.*)

Because if he's to answer to the law,
He's got a sorry lot to answer for,
Which I am about to accuse him of.
A citizen, a man of property,
Is he? Let me tell you, he has a name
Not all that different from mine in town.

We do business as we have to, to live,
Not as we, given a choice, would like to.
He backs the boxer Mennês. Me, I back
The wrestler Aristophon, as is known.
Now this Mennês has won a match or two,
Aristophon can squeeze a breath out yet,
I kid you not. See if you recognize
This Mennês afterdark, but believe me
I will be escorted, rest you assured.

(*Waggles eyebrows. Realizes that he has strayed far from what he ought
to be saying. Collects thoughts, takes aim, and gets back to his subject.*)

Thales' plea, no doubt, is going to be
He brought a cargo of wheat from Akês
Back when we had the famine. Fine and good!
I import girls from Tyros. How is this
With the people? He did not bring them wheat
And *give* it to them. Nor are my girls free.
He seems to think they are though, free gratis.
If he means, because he crosses the sea,
Because he wears a coat costs three hundred
In Attika, if he means, while I wear
This thin old shirt and these worn-out sandals
And keep house on the dry land, if he means
He can get away with forcing a girl
Behind my back, in the middle of the night,
Me sound asleep for hours in my bed,
To run away with him, then I submit
This city's no longer safe to live in.
No, not safe to live in, our proud city!
Where then is all our boasting and boosting?
He undermines us, this Thales, who should,
Like me, know his place, keep to his level,
Like me, respectful to all citizens.

(*Shakes his head sadly.*)

Such is not the case. The real uppercrust,
People with a name, they obey the laws.

They don't get me out of bed at midnight,
They don't beat me up, set fire to my house,
Haul off one of my girls against her will.
But this wildman Phrygian calling himself
Thales, whose name, gentlemen, used to be
Artimmês, has done all of the above,
Scoffing the law and the magistracy.
Now if you please, Clerk of Court, read us all
The law on assault. Let's have the timer
Plug the water clock while he reads it out,
Or

    (*Making a joke, very sure of himself.*)

    it'll look, as the man said, as if
He's put his bladder down for a carpet.

CLERK OF COURT

(*Actor has only to stand straight, assume a voice of wheezy public recti-
tude, and read from an imaginary scroll.*)

Whensoever any freeman shall do . . .

BATTAROS

(*Taking over, from memory. He has done his homework.*)

. . . a mischief unto a female slave or
Belabor her with improper intent,
His fine therefor shall be double the fine
For assault. These, gentlemen, are the words
Of Khairondas in the Code, not the words
Of one Battaros, plaintiff, bringing suit
Against one Thales, so called, defendant.
Likewise, if any man beat down a door
His fine must be no less than a mina.
And if any man set fire to a house
Or break into and enter same, his fine
Shall be one thousand drakhmas, damages
Twice that. Khairondas in the code lays down

The laws for running a city, but you,
Thales, what do you care for any law?
One day you're off in Brikindera,
Another, in Abdera. Tomorrow,
If you could get passage, you would be off
To Phaselis. And I, to speak bluntly
And to not wear out your ears, gentlemen,
And get to the point, I have been done by
Thales like the mouse in the tar bucket.
I have been hit by his fist. My front door,
Which put me back four obols to have set,
Charged to my rent the month I had it up,
Is split, and my lintel is scorched and charred.
And—come here, Myrtalê, come testify—

(*Actor leads forward an imaginary girl.*)

Let the court see you. Don't be bashful now.
All these people, look, are trying your case.
Think of them as your fathers and brothers.

(*Indignantly, to the court.*)

Would you look, gentlemen, at her torn dress.

(*Lifts her dress.*)

Look her all over, see how she is bruised
And manhandled by this ape of a man.
He has pulled every hair out of her thing!
Plucked her clean as a chicken! Were I young—
He can be thankful for my age—he would
Have breathed his own blood, I can promise you,

(*Dramatic pause.*)

Like Philippos the Locust of Samos.

(*Pause, to follow this classical allusion with meaningful silence, which does not achieve the effect intended.*)

You can laugh?

(With a furious and futile look, soon abandoned for desperate honesty.)

So I am a pederast.
I admit it. My name is Battaros.
Sisymbras my grandfather before me
And Sisymbriskos my father were both,
As I am, in the whorehouse business.

(Ranting.)

If I were stronger, I'd choke a lion
If, by Zeus, the lion's name was Thales!

(Recovers himself, rearranges his thoughts. Turns to Thales, pointing at him.)

Like as not, let's say, you love Myrtalê,
Nothing at all peculiar about that.
Me, I love a square meal. I get the one,
You get the other. That's only business.
You're feeling horny, that's natural.
What you do is pay Battaros the price
And you can bash what you've bought as you will.

(Turns to the judges.)

One point more, gentlemen, and this for you,
Not him. There were, you know, no witnesses.
You must judge this case on the face of it.
If all Thales wanted was to beat up
A poor slave and wants her to testify
Under torture, then I will take her place.
Willingly! But he must pay just the same
If he hurts me, just as if I were her.
Did Minos balance this case on his scales,
Could he try it a better way than this?
To sum up, gentlemen: if you decide
For me, it will not be for Battaros
But for all businessmen not citizens.

(Finger in air, orating.)

Now's the time to show the mettle of Kos,
Of great Merops and his proud daughter Kos!
Glory of Thessalos and Herakles!
The place Asklepios came from Trikka!
The Place where Phoibé gave birth to Leto!
Ponder all this, bring in a right judgement,
And unless all that we've heard about Phrygians
Is wrong, he will be improved by the lash.

(*Bows low, with sweep of hand, and a smirk.*)

III. The Schoolmaster

(*The actor is dressed as a harridan of a mother much given to fist-shaking, pointing, and standing aggressively with hands on hips. The skit begins with her stabbing a finger at the schoolmaster Lampriskos while holding her truant son Kottalos by an ear. We must imagine that the scene is before a school, with statues of the Muses flanking the entrance. Their presence is indicated by oaths throughout. The mother's voice is loud, distraught, vibrant, grating.*)

METROTIMÉ
If, Lampriskos, you have any respect
For decency and order in your school,
Beat this lazy lout across the shoulders
Till his last breath is about to come out!
It's the price of the roof over our head
That he has just lost spinning pennies.
Oh no! No knucklebones for this noodle!

(*Gives three painful tugs on the boy's ear, glares at him.*)

The fact of the matter is, Lampriskos,
He's already at his age a gambler
And a punk and probably something worse.
I doubt that he knows his way here to school,

Although I do, sadly, every month's end
When I come to pay you his tuition,
With good King Nannakos' tears down my cheeks
Weeping before the gods for his people.

(*Stares Lampriskos down with this piece of proverbial lore. Looks at her
son as if to pity his oafish ignorance.*)

To that den of jerks and contraband slaves
With its nonstop crapgame, that way he knows,
And how to lead others there, the rascal.
I'm tired of picking up his wax tablet
From where he throws it down against the wall
Beside his bed when he comes in from school.
And what's written on it? Nothing, nothing.
It's as clean as when I waxed it for him.
Except when, having scrawled Hades on it,
He scrapes it down to keep me from seeing.
His knucklebones lie untouched in his bag
As bright as the cruet on the table.
He cannot recognize the letter A
No matter how many times I've showed him
When, day before yesterday, his father
Spelled him *Maron*, the poor fool wrote *Simon!*
I could kick myself for not raising him
To be a caretaker of jackasses
Instead of to read and write, in fond hope
That he could support me in my old age.
But when asked to say something from a play,
As anybody might ask a schoolboy,
Whenever I ask him, or his father,
Whose eyesight is failing, and his hearing,
What trickles out, as if from a cracked jug?
Apollo the bright, a hunter was he!
Your old granny, I say, can recite that
Without being able to read or write,
Nerd, or any Phrygian slave in the street.
But dare criticize this brat one grumble
And for three days you don't lay eyes on him.

Off to Granny's! She is well up in years,
And though she has to live close to the bone,
He goes through her cupboard like a famine.
Or, up on our roof and breaking the tiles,
Sits gazing between his legs like an ape.
You see what all this does to me, clearly.
How I suffer. Broken tiles to think of,
Winter's coming, tiles cost three *himaitha*,
My eyes water to ponder the expense.
All the apartments know well who did it.

(*Renewed outrage, harder pulls on the ear.*)

Kottalos, Metrotimé's imp, is who!
I don't dare show a tooth to deny it.

(*Still pinching an ear, lifts Kottalos' shirt.*)

Would you look at his back! It looks like bark!
This is what comes of lolling in the woods
Idle as a Delian with trap seines out.
Throws his life away! He can calculate
Feast days better than an astrologer.
He can do that in his sleep.

(*Hands on hips, grim.*)

                              As you hope,
Lampriskos, for fine favors from the gods,
Give this scapegrace no fewer than . . .

(*Actor changes matron's wig for thatchy one of a schoolmaster, hooks on a
beard, and dons a wrinkled and patched cloak. His voice is full of bleats
and clipped exactnesses of pronunciation.*)

LAMPRISKOS
No more, Metrotimé, I beg of you.
He will get what he deserves. Euthiês!

(*Snaps bony fingers as he calls.*)

Kokkalos! Phillos! Report here to me.
Up with Kottalos now on your shoulders.

(*Bares Kottalos' bottom with professional detachment.*)

It is time we gazed, like Akesaios,
On the full of the moon, oh dear me, yes.
And hasn't our deportment been lovely?
Too good, Kottalos, to throw knucklebones?
Too big for our schoolmates, we must go dice
With the toughs, mustn't we? But we'll learn.
I shall make you as placid as a girl
Who never budges so much as a straw.
Hand me the oxtail whip, the one that bites,
The one I use for the hardened cases.
Be quick, before I choke on my own bile.

KOTTALOS

(*Actor lies across a stool and wiggles his legs and makes frantic movements with his arms. Voice cracks to falsetto every other phrase.*)

No! No! Please, Lampriskos, by the Muses,
By the beard on your chin, by my own life,
Not the oxtail! Beat me with the other!
Have mercy on your little Kottalos.

LAMPRISKOS
You are a rotten boy, my Kottalos.
What could I find good to say about you
Even if I were auctioning you off?
And I doubt that I could give you away
In the country where the mice eat iron.

KOTTALOS
How many lashes, how many lashes
Do I get, Lampriskos?

LAMPRISKOS
                    Ask her, not me.

KOTTALOS
Tatai! How many then, the two of you?

METROTIMÉ
I mean to live to be old. As many
As your miserable hide can last through.

(*Lampriskos flogs.*)

KOTTALOS
Quit, quit. O Lampriskos! Enough! Enough!

LAMPRISKOS
Will *you* quit gambling and playing the fool?

KOTTALOS
Yes! Yes! Never again, O Lampriskos,
I swear it by the Muses at the door.

LAMPRISKOS
What an awful lot of tongue you can flap.
One more squeal and I gag you with the mouse.

KOTTALOS
I'm silent, listen. Watch it! Don't kill me!

LAMPRISKOS

(*Whistling the oxtail whip around his head.*)

Turn him loose, Kokkalos. That should do it.

METROTIMÉ
Don't stop now with the beating, Lampriskos.
Flog on till the sun goes down, I beg you.
He's slippier by far than the Hydra.
More! He will only pretend to study.

LAMPRISKOS
No more.

METROTIMÉ
          Twenty more. If he learns to read
better than Klio, he needs twenty more.

KOTTALOS

(*Sticks out his tongue at his mother.*)

LAMPRISKOS
Go coat your tongue with honey, silly boy.

METROTIMÉ
On second thought, Lampriskos, once he's home
I'll get his old father to hobble him.
He'll be hopping with his hands and feet tied
Next time you see him, disgracing these Muses.
Their cold stares can feast on him in his straps.

IV. Women at the Temple

(*The actor wears an important, richly figured dress, and is cowled with a long shawl. This costume serves for both the women he portrays, as they are dressed for a sacrifice at the temple of Asklepios, god of healing. He uses a different voice for each, an assured, superior voice for Kynno, a rather giddy and rattling voice for Kokkalé her companion, whom she treats as an equal when she remembers to, but as an inferior by instinct. They are accompanied by a dull servant girl who does not speak. To be the Custodian, a temple attendant of minor rank, the actor sheds the long shawl, slips into a long-sleeved linen robe, hooks on a beard, and carries a staff.*)

KYNNO
(*On her knees before an imaginary altar, arms held high and wide in the traditional attitude of supplication. The prayer she recites is formulaic*

for eleven lines and then becomes a mixture of the spontaneous and
religious catchphrases.)

Rejoice, Great Paiêon, Lord of Thikka,
Whose sweet home is Kos and Epidauros,
Hail Mother Koronis and Apollon!
And her in your right hand, Hygieia!
Hail the holy altars of Panaké
And of Epio and of Iêso,
Of Podaleiros and Makhaon who
Tore down Leomedon's walls and mansion
And can heal the fiercest of diseases,
And of all gods and goddesses residing,
Father Paiêon, with you on your hearth.
Bless me, please, for the gift of this rooster.
He was the herald on my garden fence.
I am not rich, and my well is shallow.
Otherwise I would bring an ox or pig,
A fat pig, instead of this plain rooster,
In thanksgiving for the cure, O Great Lord,
Which you brought to me with your healing hands.

(*To her companion.*)

Put the dish there on Hygieia's right,
Kokkalé.

KOKKALÉ

(*Complying, piously. She admires the effect of the dish of roast rooster on*
the altar. Her eyes wander. She steps back, taking in the temple.)

      O! dear Kynno, turn around.
Look what beautiful statuary's here.
I wonder what sculptor cut this figure,
And who commissioned it to be placed here?

KYNNO
The sons of Praxiteles. Don't you see
The lettering on the base? Euthiês,
Prexon's son, see, gave it to the temple.

KOKKALÉ

(*Rather overdoing art appreciation.*)

Paiêon bless them, and bless Euthiês too,
For such beautiful work. See, dear, the girl
Gazing right up at that apple so rapt.
I think she will faint if she can't get it.

(*Bustling about, pointing.*)

And there, Kynno, that old man. Oh! but wait,

(*Discovering an Eros Straddling a Swan.*)

By the Fates, that small boy is choking a goose!
It's real! You would swear that it could speak
Were you not close enough to see it's stone.

(*Babbling.*)

The time will come when men will find how to
Put life in stone. Look at the step she takes,
This Batalé,

             (*Stooping to read.*)

             daughter of Myttes, here.

(*Sententiously.*)

If you've never seen Batalé herself,
See this, and you won't need to see Batalé!

KYNNO
To see as stunning a statue, my dear,
As you will see in your life, come with me.

(*To her servant.*)

Kydilla, go fetch the Custodian.

(*Kydilla, enthralled by the statues, pays her no attention.*)

I'm talking to you! Gawking and gaping!
Pays no more attention than a statue!

(*Indignantly shouting.*)

So stand there and stare at me like a crab!
Fetch us, I'm saying, the Custodian.
You are as helpless here in the temple,
Idiot, as in the kitchen or street.
I ask the god to witness, Kydilla,
That you are fanning my temper just when
I can't afford to blow up in a fit.
Go on, scratch your head like a simpleton.
I'll give you a reason to *hold* your head!

KOKKALÉ
Don't upset yourself for nothing, Kynno.
She's only stupid. All slaves are stupid.

KYNNO
But they're already opening the doors.
The temple will be full in just a bit.

KOKKALÉ
Aren't you looking, dear Kynno, at all
These grand works of art? These now, you could say,
Are Athene's work, bless her holy name.

(*Making on, with gestures, before a painting.*)

That naked boy there, look, I could pinch him
And leave a welt. His warm flesh is so bright .
That it shimmers like sunlight on water.
And his silver fire tongs, wouldn't Myllos
Send his eyes out on stalks in wonderment,
Or Lamprion's son Pataikiskos try
To steal them! For they are indeed that real!
The ox, the herd, and the girl who's with them,
The hooknosed man with his hair sticking up,
They are as real as in everyday life.
If I weren't a lady, I might scream
At the sight of that convincing big ox
Watching us out of the side of his eye.

KYNNO

(*Realizing that Kokkalé's art criticism is entirely to* trompe l'oeil *effects.*)

The style of Apelles the Ephesian
Is true, my dear, whatever his subject.
He painted everything equally well.
Whatever caught his imagination
He painted straight off, and to perfection.
To look at his paintings and not admire
Ought to be punished with being hung up
By the feet in a shop.

(*Sees Custodian coming.*)

Ah, here he is.

CUSTODIAN

(*Aiming to please.*)

Ladies, your sacrifice was propitious,
And liturgically correct as well.
Surely Paiêon was very well pleased.

(*Piously, lifting his staff.*)

Let us pray. O blessed Paiêon, O
Look with favor on these thy worshipers,
And on their husbands, blessed Paiêon,
And on all their kin. May this come to pass.

KYNNO
Amen. So be it, O Greatest! May we
Return in health to sacrifice again,
With worthier offerings, and with us
Bring our husbands and children.

(*Pointedly.*)

Kokkalé,
Carve a drumstick for the Custodian,
And give the snake a morsel, quietly,

(with unctuous knowledge of the ritual)

In sacred silence, there on the altar.

(Briskly.)

We'll eat, don't forget, the rest at home.

(To the Custodian.)

Stay well, my fellow. Here now, have some bread.
We'll begin with you, close to the god,
In passing it around on the way home.

V. The Jealous Woman

*(The actor has four parts: a mature matron named Bitinna; her slave
and bedmate Gastron, who is young, and whose name, Stomach, alludes
not to his body but to his sensual appetite; her servant Kydilla who is the
same age as her daughter; and an older slave Pyrrhiês, whose two lines of
dialogue do not need a costume change. A wig and a stole are sufficient to
make the actor into Bitinna, a raucous and furious woman. Beneath the
stole is a slave's smock that will do for both Gastron and Kydilla. The only
prop is a rope, which the actor tangles around himself to be Gastron tied
up.)*

BITINNA

(In a rage.)

Out with it, Gastron! You are tired of me,
So full of my legs wide open in bed
You're sniffing Menon's Amphytaiê!

GASTRON   ·
Me? Amphytaiê! I've never even
Seen her. Who is she?

BITINNA
                    New lies every day!

GASTRON

(*Doing the engaging sulk of a spoiled male.*)

Bitinna, you own me. Own my body!
Day and night you drink my blood, yes you do.

BITINNA

(*Enraged the more.*)

What a lot of tongue on you! Kydilla!
Where's Pyrrhiês? Go tell him I want him.

PYRRHIÊS

(*From another part of the house.*)

What is it?

BITINNA

(*Pointing to Gastron, fire in her eyes, singing her words.*)

       Tie him up—don't just stand there!
The well rope. Go get it. Tie him with it.

(*To Gastron.*)

If I don't make an example of you,
I'll not answer to the name of woman.
I'm a Phrygian if I don't make up for
Being fool enough to let you in my bed
As a somebody. Once a fool, twice wise.

(*To Pyrrhiês.*)

Strip him, be quick, and bind him hand and foot.

GASTRON

(*On his knees.*)

No, Bitinna, no! I beg you, don't, please.

BITINNA
Strip him, I tell you.

(*To Gastron.*)

You need reminding
That I bought you, you slave, for three minas.
Damn the day you turned up here. Pyrrhiês!

(*Pointing sarcastically.*)

You call that tying up! Start all over.
What a fool. Bind his elbows behind him
So tight the rope saws his skin if he squirms.

GASTRON
Forgive me, Bitinna! I cheated once.
I gave in to her because I'm a man.
Men can't help it. I'll let you tattoo me
If I do it again.

BITINNA
                    You waste your breath.
Save your slick words for your Amphytaiê
While you're rolling with her, thinking me
To be the doormat where you wipe your feet.

PYRRHIÊS
There! Well bound.

BITINNA
                    See that he can't wiggle loose.
And now drag him, trussed up as you have him,
Off to Hermon the executioner,
Who is to beat him a thousand lashes
Across his back, and a thousand lashes
Across his stomach.

GASTRON

(*Naked, in a tangle of rope.*)

                    Will you kill me, then,
Bitinna, before proving me guilty?

BITINNA
Didn't you just beg me to forgive you?
Bitinna, forgive me. My ears heard you.

GASTRON
I said that only to cool your temper.

BITINNA

(*In a fury, to Pyrrhiês.*)

What are you standing there and staring at?
Do what I tell you to do! Kydilla!
Whop this clod on the snout. And you, Drekhon,
Go along with them to see they get there.

(*Frantically, on the crest of her anger.*)

Take that rag, Kydilla, tie it around
His hips to hide the bastard's little dick
As he's dragged naked through the marketplace.
A thousand here,

                    (*Whacks his back.*)

               and a thousand more here.

(*Pokes his belly with her toe.*)

Repeat that, hear, Pyrrhiês, to Hermon.
Make sure you do, or be prepared to pay
Debt plus interest with your own backside.
Get on with it. Don't go by Mikkalê's
For a short cut. Right down the highway!

(*Fumes. Paces. Imagines with gleaming eyes. Smiles with wicked satis-
faction. Her blood boils and she relishes the steam. Pause. Face drains of
expression. Reason steals back from banishment.*)

I'm not thinking! Call them back, Kydilla.
Call them back, slave! Before they get too far.

KYDILLA

(*Hollering through her hands.*)

Pyr-rhi-ês! Come back! Are you deaf? Come back!

(*No response from down the road.*)

Damn! He's dragging him along like a sack.
He treats him as if he was a robber,
And him his buddy! Pyrrhiês! You lout!
You like bullying him tied up like that,
Don't you, dragging him off to be tortured.
These two eyes will see you not five days off
Sporting Akhaian chains on your ankles.
Antidoros has fitted them on you
At the smithy before, and will again.
It's not that long since you were wearing them.

BITINNA

(*To Pyrrhiês.*)

You! Bring him back, keep him tied, dump him here.
Go fetch Kosis and his tattoo needles,
And his ink.

(*To Gastron.*)

        He will decorate your hide
All over and make the one job of it,
Without let or stint, hanging, trussed, and gagged,
Like any proud Davos of a butler.

KYDILLA

(*Interfering boldly.*)

No, please, Missy, just this one time be kind.
Give a thought to Batyllis, her wedding,
Sweet grandbabies to dandle on your lap.
For this happy thought pardon him this once.
I beg you.

BITINNA
                         Quit pestering, Kydilla,
Before I boot you one out of the house.

(*Draws herself to full height and quivers.*)

Let this slave seven times over get off!
No, the world would be right to spit in my face.
No, by the Great Mother of us all, no.
He cannot help being a man, he says.
He knows that much, and he will know some more
When we, to remind him he is a man,
Tattoo KNOW THYSELF all over his face.

KYDILLA

(*Counting on her fingers.*)

The Gerenia is only four days off!

(*Happy to have remembered a religious law.*)

Today's the twentieth. You can't . . .

BITINNA

(*Thwarted, and perhaps welcoming a way out.*)

                                        Yes, well.

(*With a patient sigh.*)

I'll let you escape this once. You can thank
Kydilla for it. If she can get around me,
It is because I raised her in these arms.
I love her as I love my Batyllis,
Like a daughter.

                         (*Grimly, savoring a new revenge.*)

                 After the festival,
After we have drunk to the sleeping dead,
You can look forward to as much pleasure

As theirs, day after day, my fine fellow.
You have tasted your last of the honey.

(*Snaps her fingers in haughty triumph.*)

VI. A Private Talk Between Friends

(*The actor impersonates two women seated on stools. He has but to switch
from one stool to the other and change shawls of distinctive design to be
alternately the two. Their shoes should be in fashion, and their conversa-
tion that of women of the world in the swim of things.*)

KORITTO

(*Welcoming her friend, who has come to visit.*)

Do have a seat, Metro.

(*Realizes that there is none. Wheels on her servant girl, shouting and
making hysterical gestures with her arms.*)

                              Get up! A stool
For this lady! Must I say what to do
Or you don't lift a finger? Is that it?
Are you some kind of rock, or a servant?
The liveliness of a corpse! Except, of course,
When I measure out your ration of meal.
You count the grains. If I spill a little,
You grumble and pout until I wonder
The walls don't sigh in sympathy, and fall.

(*Ominous pause. Finds new angle of attack.*)

Just now wiping the stool clean, aren't you?
And why, pray, hasn't it been kept dusted?
You can be very thankful there's a guest,
Else wouldn't you taste the flat of my hand!

METRO

(*Sympathetically, complacently.*)

We wear the same yoke, my dear Koritto.
I have to bark like a dog day and night
At these lazy and unspeakable oafs.

(*Pulls her stool closer.*)

What I've come about . . .

KORITTO

(*Suddenly jumps up and runs toward servants, flapping her dress.*)

Out from underfoot, all you shiftless sluts!
You sneaks and gossips! All ears and tongues
And nothing else to you but idle butts!

(*Sits. Composes herself.*)

METRO

(*Tries again.*)

                              You must tell me now,
Koritto dear, who made you your dildo,
The beautifully stitched red leather one.

KORITTO

(*Agape with surprise.*)

But how now, when, where can you have seen it?

METRO

Erinna's daughter had it given her
Day before yesterday, Nossis, you know.
What a beautiful present for a girl.

KORITTO

(*Befuddled and alarmed.*)

Nossis? Who gave it to her?

METRO

                              If I tell,
Will you tell on me?

KORITTO

(*Touching eyelids with fingers.*)

                              These sweet eyes, Metro!
Koritto's mouth lets out naught.

METRO

                              Eubylé,
Bitas' wife, gave it to her. Promised her,
What's more, nobody would be the wiser.

KORITTO
Women! That woman will uproot me yet.
I let her have it because she begged me.
Metro, I hadn't yet used it myself!
And she treats it like something she has found,
And makes an improper present of it.
Goodbye and goodbye to a friend like her,
Is what I say. She can find other friends.
She has lent my property to Nossis!
Adresteia forgive me for speaking
Stronger than a woman should. But Nossis!
I wouldn't give her my old worn-out one
Even if I still had a thousand more.

METRO
Now, now, Koritto. Keep your dander down.
Better to enjoy an even temper.
I shouldn't have babbled. I talk too much.
It would be an improvement all around
Were I to lose my tongue. But, to get back,
Who did make it? Do tell me, as a friend.

(*Taken aback a bit.*)

Why are you looking at me so funny?
I'm Metro, not a stranger, after all.
What is this prudishness? Be a sport, now.
Who's the craftsman that made it? What's his name?

KORITTO

(*Laughing.*)

What a pitiful plea! Kerdon made it.

METRO
Which Kerdon? The grey-eyed one, the Kerdon
Who's Kylaithis' Myrtalinê's neighbor?
He couldn't make a plectrum for a harp.
Near Hermodoros' apartment house
Off Main Street, there's another, somebody
In his day but getting old, I would think.
He used to do it with Pylaithis when
She was living. Gone but not forgotten,
Poor dear, if her kin ever think of her.

KORITTO
Neither of those, Metro, as you've figured.
This one is Khian or Erythraian,
One or the other, baldheaded and little.
He is the spit image of Prexinos
But talks altogether different, though.
He does his work at home behind closed doors,
You never know where revenue spies lurk.
Real Khoan, his stitching and polishing.
You'd think Athena had done it, not Kerdon.
Well, I—he brought me two of them, Metro—
I thought my eyes would pop out with staring.
I can tell you this, we are all alone,
No man was ever hung like these beauties,
So long and stiff, and as smooth as a dream,

And the leather straps are as soft as wool.
What a godsend to women, this cobbler!

METRO
Why didn't you buy the other one too?

KORITTO
What didn't I do to get it, Metro!
I tried every persuasion, I kissed him,
Fondled his bald head, gave him a sweet drink,
Called him my pet, tickled his hairy ears,
Everything but open my legs to him.

METRO
But you should have, if that's what he wanted.

KORITTO
Yes, but I really didn't have the chance.
Bitas' Euboulé was here grinding meal
On my millstone, as she does day and night,
Wearing it out, I'll need a new one soon,
I swear, Bitas being too tightfisted
To spend four obols for one of his own.

METRO
How did he know to come here, Koritto?
Don't fib.

KORITTO
            Artemis sent him, Kandas' wife,
She showed him my house.

METRO
                        Aiei! Artemis,
She's always into things, more than Thallo,
Especially with anything sexy.
But if he wouldn't sell you both of them,
Didn't you ask who ordered the other?

KORITTO
Yes I did. He wasn't about to tell.
Somebody he hopes to seduce, I'll vow.

METRO

(*Rising, arranging her shawl for the street.*)

Well, I think I'd better be leaving you.
I just might happen upon Artemis
And find out when I can find Kerdon in.

(*Blows a kiss.*)

Wish me luck, Koritto.

(*Breaks into a salacious grin.*)

                        A sweet longing
Buzzes around in a certain person.

(*Leaves.*)

KORITTO

(*To a servant.*)

Go close the front door, you fool of a girl,
And then go count the chickens in the yard,
And throw them some darnel while you're there.
People steal anything nowadays, for sure,
Even your pet hen and her on your lap.

VII. The Shoemaker

(*The actor wears a cobbler's smock over which he can put an ample stole to be his customer Metro, as hard-to-get-along-with a shopper as ever drove a shoe clerk to distraction. The women who have come with Metro can be indicated by gestures toward them, nudges, winks, and smirks.*)

METRO

(*Expansively, with middle-class condescension toward an inferior.*)

Kerdon, I bring you these women friends here
To look at some of your beautiful work.

KERDON

(*Overdoing it, as with all his fawning.*)

No wonder, Metro, I'm your admirer!

(*To a servant.*)

Put the settle outside for these ladies.

(*Nothing happens.*)

It's you I mean, Drimylos. Are you deaf?
Asleep again!

(*To another servant.*)

Hit him on the nose, you!
Pistos! Kick the sleep out of that sad lout!
The behind! The neck! Twist both his arms off!

(*To Drimylos.*)

Up, you scoundrel! We can make it rougher.

(*Seethes. More scandal.*)

Dusting the bench, are you, at this late date?
Why, you white-assed punk, wasn't it kept clean?
I'll dust your seat, just you wait, with a plank.

(*To the women.*)

Be seated, Metro, do.

(*To a servant.*)

That cabinet,
Pistos, open it up. No, not that one,
The other one up there on the third shelf.

Bring us those beauties here. What luck, Metro!
What shoes you're going to see.

(*To Pistos.*)

                              Careful,
You pig, with that showcase.

(*To the women.*)

                              This shoe, Metro,
Perfectly shaped from various leathers,
Is a dandy. See, ladies, these firm soles,
These neat straps, the rounding off of the toe.
Nothing shoddy anywhere, all first rate.
Take the color, now—may Pallas answer
Your heart's prayer for the shoe of your dreams—
You won't find such color at the dyer's,
Nor yet such shine in an artist's beeswax.
Cost three minas day before yesterday,
That pair did, from Kandas the wholesaler,
And a pair like them, I tell you the truth,
On my word, there is no point in lying,
I hope never to prosper in business
If he didn't say he was giving me
These items as a personal favor,
So to speak, what with the price of leather
Going up everyday at the tanners.
A work of art's what you'll be buying,
Practically stealing it from my poor hands.
Night and day I wear out my bench working,
No time to eat, even, until sunset.
The din is worse than Mikion's wild beasts.
Not to mention the thirteen slaves I need,
Lazy dogs, the lot of them, they are too.
Business falls off a bit, and all you hear
Out of them is *Give me this, give me that.*
Business is brisk, they roost around like hens
Keeping their between the legs good and warm.

(Realizing that his digression isn't selling shoes.)

You can't spend promises on anything,
As they say: cash on the barrel for these,
Or for as good a pair, we have lots more.
We'll keep showing until you're pleased.
Bring out all the cabinets here, Pistos.
What a pity if you don't find a pair.
But you will. Look here. There is every style:
Sikonian and Ambrakidian,
Nossises, Khian, parrots and hemp soles,
Saffron mules and around the house slippers,
Ionian button tops and night walkers,
High ankles, crab claws, Argeian sandals,
Cockscombs, cadets, flat heels. Just tell me now.
Ladies, what's your heart's desire. Speak right out.
Women and dogs, as we all know, eat shoes.

METRO
How much are you asking for that first pair?
And don't talk such a storm, you'll drive us
Out of your shop with all this jabbering.

KERDON

(Unfazed, inured to nattering women.)

Price it yourself, dear madam, whatever
You think is just, or this pair, or this.
What's fairer than that? How could I cheat you
If I let you set the value yourself?
If you know true work, make me an offer.
May a fox make its den in my grey hair,
My hair grey as ashes, if I don't sell you
Fine shoes today and eat well tomorrow.

(Aside, to the audience, hamming his lines like a traditional villain, rubbing his greedy hands.)

Hermes the Fox and Peitho the Vixen!
I shall haul something in for supper
With this cast of the net, or know why not!

METRO

Why do you mutter and ramble on so
And not give the price with an honest tongue?

KERDON

Look high, look low, this pair is a mina.
Ladies, if you were Pallas Athena
The price would be the same, not a cent less.

METRO

(*Her patience gone, fire in her eye.*)

I see now why your cabinets are full,
Kerdon. Works of art, indeed, that you keep
For yourself, clearly not for customers.

(*Archly.*)

The twentieth of Taureon, you know,
Is Hekatê's daughter Artakenê's
Wedding, for which new shoes will be needed.
They will all come here, I am sure they will,
So you'd better get a sack for a purse
For what they'll spend, and you can dread thieves.

KERDON

(*Unimpressed.*)

For Hekatê as for Artakenê
The price is still a mina, be assured,
As it is for you, when you make your choice.

METRO

(*With practiced sarcasm.*)

Is it not your luck, Kerdon, to touch
Charming feet which love and desire have touched,
And you the scab off of a running sore?

(*Looks around among her friends, pleased with herself, for having put this scum of a merchant in his place. Moves in on Kerdon for the kill.*)

Now you can, you think, manipulate me,
But not my friend here. What will you charge her
For that pair? Think again before you speak.

KERDON

(*Undaunted, brassy as ever.*)

Five staters, by the gods, are offered me
Daily by Eveteris the psaltrist
For that pair, but I wouldn't sell them to her
If she were to make the price four darics.
She flits around making fun of my wife
And she can go barefoot for all I care.

(*Changing tactics while he has the upper hand.*)

If you indeed want them, take these three pairs,
But for nothing less than seven darics.
I couldn't dream of it. Seven darics.

(*Leaps to fill the vacuum of their hesitation.*)

How could I deny you, Metro, anything?

(*Smiling foxily.*)

You, Metro, whose voice lifts me to the gods,
A shoemaker, a very stone, you lift.

(*Imagines he is quoting from poetical speeches he has heard at the theatre.*)

For your tongue is not a tongue but a whisk
For delights. Like one of the gods is he,
Ah! who hears you talking day in day out!

(*Squats, a shoe in his hand.*)

Stick your tiny foot out now and let me
Slip this shoe on it.

(*Throws up hands in wonderment.*)

                    Fits to perfection!
What possible improvement could you want?

(*Quotes again, finger beside nose.*)

Beautiful things belong to the beautiful!
You would think that Athena made this shoe.

(*Quickly, to another woman.*)

You, if you please, your foot.

(*Removes her shoe and holds it up for all to see.*)

                    What! Did an ox
Make you this shoe, imitating its hoof?

(*Fits on one of his shoes.*)

If my knife had followed your foot's outline,
Could the fit of this shoe have been nicer?
By my household altar, it's perfect!

(*To another woman, who is already leaving.*)

You at the door snickering like a horse
At me and my wares, seven darics now,
And this pair is all yours, what do you say?

(*The women are all gathering themselves to leave, having seen every shoe
in the place.*)

Well, you need sandals for around the house.
Or bedroom slippers. So just send a slave.

(*On a hopeful note.*)

Remember, Metro, red shoes by the ninth,
In good time for the wedding, keep in mind.

(*Proverbially.*)

Winter clothes must be made in summer heat.

(*Looks heavenward in disgust.*)

VIII. The Dream

[A COMIC POET]

(*To his servants.*)

Get up, Psylla! Get up, girl. If you snooze
The whole day away, who's to slop the pig?
She's out there famished, grunting for breakfast.
Are you waiting for the sun to come up!
A nine-year night would be too short for you!
You sleep so hard it makes you tired. Get up!
Light the lamps. Put the pig out to pasture.
She's driving me crazy. Grumble and scratch!

(*Pokes the slave Psylla with a stick.*)

There! Next time I'll dint your lazy head.
Megallis! You in the Latmian cave?
You're everlastingly tired, O yes.
But certainly not tired from carding wool.
I need a strand now for a sacrifice
And there's not a wisp anywhere about.
Get up, you rascal!

(*To a slave already up and about.*)

                    Anna, a moment
With you, please. You are my one sane servant.
Come listen to a dream I had last night.
[   ]
I was dragging a goat down a gully,

A fine goat with big horns and a long beard,
And when [   ] from the wood
[   ] for I was driven back
[   ] goatherds [   ]
[   ]
But I didn't dare [   ]
And to another oak tree [   ]
All around [   ]
Took the goat [   ]
And nearby me [   ]
[   ]
[   ] yellow [   ]
[   ] finely rounded [   ]
[   ] a short fawnskin tunic
[   ] cape over his shoulders
[   ] ivy garlanding his hair
[   ] boots [   ]
[   ] coat [   ]
Odysseus [   ] gift of Aiolos
[   ] kick with his heel
[   ] the best
As they do dancing to Dionysos
And then some dived headfirst into the dust,
And rolled, and some flopped wildly on their backs.
All this was both comic and pitiful,
Anna [   ]
I thought twice [   ] jumped,
Alone of them all, urged on [   ]

[*Ten lines unreadable.*]

Puffing and blowing, stamping with his foot.
Out of my sight, or, old man that I am,
I will cripple you with my walking stick!
I cried out: *O all you people, I die*
For my country if this old man hits me.
I stand well with this boy, as he will say,
[   ] the guard [   ]

Then the dream was over [   ]
Fetch me my clothes [   ]
[   ] the dream [   ]
[   ] getting the goat out of the gully
[   ] gift of handsome Dionysos
Just as the goatherds rent and ate the goat,
So do the critics savage my poems.
They kick me about before the Muses.
Here's what I think it means. I take first prize
In balancing best on the greased wineskin.
Of all those trying to keep their footing
I alone kept from falling, I alone
Aroused the old man's envy, old Hipponax.
By the Muses! The iambic Muses!
I shall take the prize for comic poems,
Master of satire in all Ionia.

IX. The Breakfast

WOMAN

Let's all sit. And where now is the baby?
Maia, hand him here. Eveteira, too.
And Glykê [   ]
[   ]
[   ]
[   ]
[   ] bring me
[   ] slut of a slave!
Bring [   ]
Put it there [   ]
The laxative mint [   ]

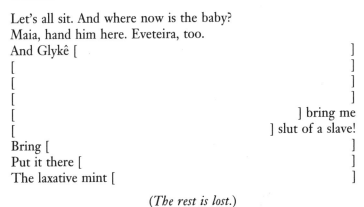

(The rest is lost.)

X. Molpinos

(*Speaker unknown.*)

You've had, Gryllos, sixty rounds of the sun.
Die now, Gryllos, and mingle with the dust.
The last turns of the track are blindly run.
Go. The light is dying, as all light must.

(*The rest is lost.*)

XI. The Working Girls

(*Speaker unknown.*)

Hugging as tight as a limpet its rock.

(*The rest is lost.*)

XII. [   ]

(*Speaker unknown.*)

A family with trouble is hard
To find. For every problem you solve,
There's another ready to take its place.

(*The rest is lost.*)

XIII. [The Little Boy]

(Speaker unknown.)

Playing blind man's bluff, banging the cookpot,
Flying a junebug tethered by a thread,
He destroyed his grandpa's afternoon nap.

(The rest is lost.)

Notes

ARCHILOCHOS

Translated from the text of Archilochos established by François Lasserre, published in 1958 by the Association Guillaume Budé, *Archiloque, Fragments, texte établi par François Lasserre, traduit et commenté par André Bonnard* (Paris), except for 18, which is the recently discovered Cologne Papyrus, and 259, which is my conjectural reading of a newly edited fragment in Sir Denys Page's *Supplementum Lyricis Graecis* (Oxford, 1974). Since I first read Archilochos in J. M. Edmonds's *Elegy and Iambus*, Vol. II (Cambridge, Mass.: Harvard University Press, 1931; reprinted 1954), the scholar will find traces of that edition in my translation, and twice I have preferred Edmonds's reading to Lasserre's.

1. Possibly a complete epigram.
4. The island is Thasos, where Archilochos's father founded a settlement.
6. A badly mangled fragment, restored by conjecture.
8. Three discrete fragments joined this way on the evidence of an underground temple to Cotytto frequented by homosexuals. Archilochos's acid remarks about hair styles turn up in several other fragments.
13. Long hair was a hazard in close fighting, as the enemy could grab it if matters came to that.
14. For the opulence of Gyges, see Herodotus.
16. Death as a gift: a prophylactic use of language common in Archilochos.
18. [S 478 Archilochus P. Colon. 7511 saec. ii p. C. prim. ed. R. Merkelbach and M. L. West, *ZPE* 1974] Composed around 650 B.C., discovered by Anton Fackelmann on papyrus used for mummy wrapping. There have been many essays on this new fragment (or poem entire), and much pedantic argument as to what's going on in it. I think it is a comic ode about a biological jumping the gun that transposes an erotically comic poem into a wholly comic one. Its humor is still native to barracks. See Peter Green, *The Times Literary Supplement*, 14 March 1975, p. 272, and H. D. Rankin, *Archilochus of Paros* (Noyes Classical Studies, 1977), pp. 57–73, and my "Archilochos: Fireworks on the Grass," *The Hudson Review* XXVIII, 3: 352–356.
26. The left quarter or fifth of a poem torn vertically.
27. Largely conjecture and restoration.
28. Bonnard gives "ear dripping blood."
29. This sounds like Courtly Love. It is rather raw sexual desire.
50. Since Demeas of Paros has explained that the imagery of the gathering storm

is from a poem about the beginning of a war, I have supplied "War, Glaukos, war!" as an extra line to the fragment.

53. From a paraphrase.

54. More literally, and more mysterious, "Having hanged themselves, they vomited their mass of pride."

58. The middle of three lines.

64. Line endings only legible.

71. Torn down both sides.

73. [334] Only the first line is Archilochos; the rest is probably an imitation (Lasserre).

75. Bonnard translates Erasmonides as "son of love."

81. "and I, I" is a conjecture of Lasserre's.

86. *Tuché* and *Moira*, Luck and Fate (or Accident and Predestination, Fortune and Destiny).

94. This is a larger fragment of 67 ("Thief and the night, Thief and the night"), a line known in Eustathius before the recovery of a papyrus version. And see Edmonds 46.

95. Both sides of the poem torn away.

99. A fragment with three mutilated words.

102. An Olympic victory chant.

105. A guess, possibly a wild one.

113. This satire was provoked by the superstitious reaction to the solar eclipse of 14 March 711 B.C.

118. This fragment has also been translated as the opening of 175.

119. An indecipherable fragment of which this is lines 14–15 only.

122. A ruin of paper and the translation neater than called for.

124. The only decipherable word among the remains of five.

125. Conjecture; scarcely legible.

126. "Calamitous" is a conjecture. "Wretched" perhaps.

136. Partly conjecture.

137. Fragment torn on both sides.

138. The Greek is simply *frog*. The context would be either a fable or an insult, hence the extension beyond lexicography.

142. Restoration by Lasserre.

144. The first line is supplied. Plutarch quotes the passage, saying that Fortune is like the woman in Archilochos who carries water in one hand, fire in the other.

145. Both sides of the poem torn away.

146. *Moeurs asiatiques.*

150. Field canteen.

152. Only the *ykide* of *Kyrikides* can be read.

161. [193] Bonnard translates this *tu n'as donc pas de coeur au ventre*; Edmonds: *for thou hast no gall to thy liver*. I don't know what it means.

166. The Greek is not as coherent as my English.

168. Falstaff at Shrewsbury.

169. Severely mutilated except for two lines. Field hospital.

173. The Greek is not as clear as the translation.

175. Only the left-hand side of the fragment exists, and a fair amount of guess-work went into stitching the sense together.

182. A conjectural restoration.

183. Translated by substituting the seven appropriate English words for the seven Greek ones. The alternate version is to suggest what seems to me to be the tone. Aesop derives from Archilochos. Ezra Pound, reading this translation in 1964, remarked of this fragment that there is a magpie in China that can turn a hedgehog over and kill it.

184. Death as a gift again. See 16.

191. Troop ship.

192. From a paraphrase.

199. The paeon is a hymn either to Apollo or to Asklepios, both gods of healing and of particular importance to soldiers.

200. A spurious fragment.

202. Badly damaged.

203. Much restored. The original, a quotation by Demeas of Paros, seems to have received a shotgun blast.

206. Same as 227 (I knocked him out the door with a vine-stump cudgel). Lasserre emended the old reading *door* to *mountain*. The verb in each means to attack with a cudgel.

209. The grotesque satire, obviously sexual, in these two fragments has generated some curious explanations. All that's certain is that the meaning is obscene.

215. [211] A "black-butted" fellow, literally.

228. Two mutilated words, one restored by Lasserre.

232. Neobulé, daughter of Lykambes.

239. "Swordsman" I've supplied, since a "son of Ares" would be a soldier.

244. Unless we count a tmesis in the *Iliad*, this is the first appearance of *panhellenic*.

250. Torn down both sides, restored by Lasserre.

251. Right side missing.

255. The same as 266. Bonnard translates: *et trancha les nerfs de son membre*; Edmonds, *fracti sunt nervi mentulae*. I give this reading at 266; the reading here was arrived at torturously and I let it stand as a signpost to all the pitfalls of translators. Plutarch remarks of the man who threw a rock at a dog and hit his mother-in-law that there's something to be said for most failures.

258. A guess.

259. A conjectural reading.

268. From a paraphrase. Hyperbole, one would think.

275. Three discrete fragments that fit together neatly.

276. Lucian's paraphrase of an unknown passage in Archilochos. Plutarch also mentions it.

279. Possibly an overtranslation. I have extended the image of the sea combed by the wind into what seems to be a permissible conceit: nostalgia, loneliness, combing, woman.

281. Birdnest supplied by conjecture.

287. Colophon. "You have taken a cricket by the wing," says the Greek, but Lucian in *The Liar* makes the context clear.

SAPPHO

Translated from Edgar Lobel and Denys Page, *Poetarum Lesbiorum Fragmenta* (Oxford: Oxford University Press, 1963).

1. *that persuasion / fetch her:* Gods, abstract concepts, and states of mind are not easily distinguishable in the Greek mind; Sappho may mean the goddess Persuasion, Peitho, daughter of Aphrodite. Sappho prefers her to her male counterpart Eros. *enlist her . . . shield:* the tight friendships of Sappho and her friends with adolescent girls seem from the military imagery to suggest a conscious parallel with that between men and boys in the Greek armies.

2. From a pottery shard. Kypris is Aphrodite.

6. Aida: Hades. Written, seemingly, to a standoffish girl. Thomas Hardy translates this in a poem called *Achtung.*

7. Dill: the aromatic herb (*anethum graveolens*), the same as we use for pickling. Its leaves, together with those of celery, were woven into garlands and worn around the head.

8. The opening lines probably mean: "I lifted up / [ ] / Gongyla," but the misreading, if misreading it be, is by this time too resonant to change, and there's nothing crucial in them to our understanding of the fragment. Hermes: Sappho sang *Ermais.*

14. The marriage of Hector and Andromache. The meter and dialect are epic. The opening lines are in ruin, but Kypris is mentioned, and the herald's name seems to be Idaos.

22. A papyrus blackened at the top and torn down the right side.

25. Elena: Helen.

26. magic liquor: nectar. *There* is emphatic, and was a way of designating the dwelling of the gods.

28. Gorgo is probably a nickname, an affectionate insult among close friends. Mary Barnard suggests the schoolgirlish *Monkeyface* as an equivalent.

29. Only the extreme left side is readable.

30. Kleïs was Sappho's mother or daughter. This song seems to have been

written during a political exile; the Kleanaktides were the hostile faction in power in Lesbos.

34. For once I take *gambros* (bridegroom, husband, son-in-law, kinsman) in its sense of *suitor*.

35. Holy goatskin: the aegis.

39. Peitho: the goddess Persuasion or Enticement.

42. Ermiona: Hermione. Elena: Helen.

44. The Muses gave the honor.

49. The butler guards the bridal chamber; the song would seem to be for the shivaree that went on all night after a wedding.

51. Aphrodite.

61. Part of the right-hand half of a poem. My opening is guesswork, based on what may be the word for an altar to Demeter.

63. The Greek contains scribe's errors and is not at all clear.

67. A satiric version of 74.

74. Same as 67, allowing for the possibility of a serious tribute, and reading *polyanaktidas* as an epithet rather than a girl's name.

75. A wedding-night song.

78. The opening line is: *I honestly wish to die.*

79. Ben Jonson was aware of this fragment and quotes it in *The Sad Shepherd* (II.vi. 85–86) as "the deare, good Angell of the Spring, / The Nightingale."

80. Hilda Doolittle gives an imaginative extension of this fragment in her poem *Fragment 113*, *Selected Poems* (New York, 1957), pp. 36–37.

84. The last line is a guess.

107. Places sacred to Aphrodite.

109. The Greek is not clear and may be a miscopying.

112. Literally, "cool the burning desire in my heart."

113. The sense is more blatantly Greek than I have been able to suggest: "He who is beautiful is beautiful only as long as he's beautiful to the eyes, but he who is also good, will be beautiful all his life."

116. After the first three lines it would seem that the song turns its attention to the bride.

118. Alkaios, Sappho's contemporary and fellow poet.

124. Sophia: mastery of a skill, intelligence, wisdom.

134. The Greek is probably miscopied, filled with wordplay and puns.

136. I.e., the nature of Aphrodite.

142. The Greek is not clear.

146. The myth of Tithonos is probably alluded to in the lines about Dawn.

151. Quoted by Aristotle.

160. Gea, the earth; Ouranos, the sky.

162. The goddess Peitho, Persuasion.

165. A description of Jason's coat.

167. Torn down both sides.

175. The names of three kinds of lyre.
181. Torn down both sides.
184. Hector.
185. Righthand side missing.
198. Or: without evil intent.
206. "some other of all mankind," says the Greek.

ALKMAN

Translated from *Alcmane: I Frammenti, Testo critico, traduzione, commentario* by
Antonio Garzya (Naples, 1954).

ANAKREON

From the Greek text as established in D. L. Page's *Pœtæ Melici Græcis: Pœtarum
Lyricorum Græcorum Fragmenta quæ Recens Innotuerunt*, with additions from J.
M. Edmonds' *Lyra Græca*, Vol. II (Harvard University Press, 1952). The poems
from Edmonds' edition are epigrams ascribed to Anakreon in *The Greek Anthol-
ogy* which Sir Denys Page thought spurious.

1. Kypris: Aphrodite.
2. The same papyrus: fragment 4. The opening image refers to boxing and
   probably comes from Anakreon's athletic-erotic imagery of wrestling, run-
   ning a race with, or playing ball with Eros.
3. The same papyrus. Pierides: the Muses.
4. Oxyrhynchos papyrus. The word for the boy's shorn head, meaning some-
   thing like *knobby*, is one used of calves' incipient horns, so I've added "as a
   calf."
5. Seven more lines of the preceding fragment, taken by Page and Fränkel to
   be from a different poem. Who "the famous woman known to all" is we no
   longer know.
6. Inscription for a statue of Artemis, perhaps.
7. Ialysos was one of the three Dorian cities on Rhodes.
8. This may also mean that footmen who quarrel are a nuisance.
9. That good-natured *kouros* Megistes: a boy old enough for military training.
12. Talents are money. Greedy Tantalos was punished in Hades by never being
    able to touch the food and drink that always receded when he reached.
14. Deunysos: Dionysos.
15. Hermann Fränkel says in his *Early Greek Poetry and Philosophy* (translated
    by Moses Hadas and James Willis, Harcourt Brace Jovanovich, 1973) that
    Eros' red ball is the earlier version of his arrows.

16. An imitation of Archilochos' satiric
    Now that Leophilos is the governor,
    Leophilos meddles in everybody's business,
    And everybody falls down before Leophilos,
    And all you hear is Leophilos, Leophilos.
    In each poem the proper name appears with case ending genitive, dative, and accusative.

18. A wish on Amalthiê's horn got you anything you wanted. Tartessos is Spain. King Arganthonios was believed to have made all his subjects happy.

19. Posideion was a month corresponding to the end of December and the beginning of January.

29. See 45: the fragment is satiric.

33. Comic hyperbole. Throwing oneself off a cliff because of unrequited love was a detail of Ionian folklore.

34. The Mysians, an ancient people mentioned by Homer as allies of the Trojans, inhabited a vague area of northeast Asian Minor. Teos, Anakreon's birthplace, was at the edge of, or just within, this territory.

41. Peitho (Persuasion, Seduction) was a sister or companion to Eros. She is prominent in Sappho, but fades away in later mythology.

55. Garlands around the neck were proper dress for a banquet.

56. Knucklebones, a game like jacks: the traditional pastime of schoolboys.

61. *Ta dikaia* (the just, proper, right things) of the beloved is in his or her beauty. The thought is Erewhonian (and Shakespearean) to our ears.

68. Greek poetry of Anakreon's time, and earlier, was convinced that does have antlers.

72. Bassarids: women celebrants of the Bacchanalia. They were dressed in fox skins. The dance described here was one in which the legs were apart, as if straddling something.

78. *Colt* or *filly:* same word for both.

100. "Mixed thighs." There's also the phrase "mingling feet."

105. The source is a speech by Protogenes in Plutarch's "Dialogue on Love" (*Moralia*, Vol. 9) in which he says that just as there is only one true eagle, Homer's Black or Hunter Eagle (other and lesser eagles lacking its nobility), so there is only one true love, that of adolescent boys, who, unlike girls, do not go around "glowing with desire" or "gleaming with spiced oil," giving Anakreon as the author of these phrases.

126. Athamas, Strabo says in his *Geography*, was the founder of Teos, Ankreon's birthplace.

136. Perhaps "the beauty of Bathyllos."

146. A simile that has become science: calyx.

149. Lydia was the trend setter for refinement in manners and styles.

151. Polykrates: ruler of Samos from 535 to 522 or thereabout. Anakreon served as his court poet. He was what we would now call a pirate.

158. An editor's note on the phrase "the beautiful bedroom" in Apollonius of
     Rhodes' *Argonautica* has survived except for his quotation from Anakreon
     which demonstrated that the beauty of things and people is not in their
     appearance but in our love for them.

HERONDAS

The translations follow the order and Greek text of I. C. Cunningham's *Herodas:
Mimiambi* (The Clarendon Press, Oxford 1971), the best and most recent edi-
tion. (I have, however, reversed XII and XIII, so as to end with the fragment
about Grandpa's nap rather than the grim one about family trouble). Whilst
working, I had before me *Herodas: The Mimes and Fragments*, with Notes by
Walter Headlam, edited by A. D. Knox (Cambridge University Press, 1966 [first
printing 1922]); *Hérondas: Mimes*, Texte établi par J. Arbuthnot Nairn et Traduit
par Louis Laloy, Paris: Société d'Édition Les Belles Lettres, 1928; and Frederic
Will's *Herondas*, Twayne World Authors Series, New York 1973.

I. THE MATCHMAKER

The setting is a house in town, probably on Kos. Time: early third century BC.

Threissa: Slaves tended to be named for their native land: this one is from Thrace.
The Goddess: Aphrodite.
Five prizes in athletics: Gryllos' achievements are meant to sound as exaggerated
     as the description of Egypt before.
Kythera: Aphrodite.
Misa: Originally a Phrygian goddess. In the myth of Demeter and Persephone,
     she persuaded Demeter to eat during her long grief. The festival parade
     would be part of the Eleusinian mysteries.
Tippy: The Greek is *Simé*, snub-nosed. Myrtle and Tippy would seem to be
     acquaintances of Gyllis with a similar bent for genteel pimping.

II. THE WHOREHOUSE MANAGER

The setting is a court of law in Kos. Battaros, the *pornoboskos* of the title, is
     arguing his case of assault and arson against Thales, a shipowner. Time:
     before 266 BC.

Akês: Seaport in Phoenicia.
Tyros: Tyre.
Attika: The region of Greece of which Athens is the great city. Battaros thinks of
     it as a fashion center.
wildman Phrygian: a racial insult.

Plug the water clock: Time for speeches in court was measured by pots of dripping water, on the principle of the hourglass. The reading of the law was on the court's time, not that allotted to Battaros. His vulgar joke is that if the attendant spills some of the water, it will look as if he has pissed.

Brikindera is in Rhodes.

Abdera is in Thrace.

Phaselis is in Lycia, and had a bad reputation for wickedness, civic corruption, and piracy.

the mouse in the tar bucket: a proverbial situation. That Battaros does not use it correctly (it should mean trouble that you brought on yourself) is part of his characterization.

He has pulled every hair out of her thing: This is *chutzpah.* Battaros is counting on the magistrates' not knowing that prostitutes depilated their pubic hair. Or is the joke that they can't afford to admit that they know?

Philippos the Locust of Samos: a boxer famous for having been strangled when his opponent twisted his long hair around his throat.

Sisymbras and *Sisymbriskos* are both kinds of mint. Flowery names were popular with whores, and, as Cunningham shows, denoted effeminacy in men; he mentions a whorehouse keeper named Hyacinth.

Minos: judge of the dead.

of great Merops: this spate of patriotic mythology is something Battaros could have heard in any political speech.

III. THE SCHOOLMASTER

The setting is a grammar school, and probably its porch, as statues of the Muses are alluded to throughout, and these would be at the entrance or around a courtyard just inside.

Nannakos: a king of the Phrygians who foresaw the flood Deukalion (the Greek Noah) survived, and wept for his people. "To weep like King Nannakos" and "to be from the time of Nannakos" (for something or someone out-of-date) were proverbial expressions.

Simon was a name for a throw of the dice.

Akesaios: the pilot of Neleus, who always sailed at the full of the moon. So the proverb means to recognize opportunity and to take it, but Lampriskos also means Kottalos' bare bottom.

the country where the mice eat iron: a country so poor the mice have nothing else to eat?

Tatai!: a cry of pain.

gag you with the mouse: the name of the gag sounds like schoolboy slang. Cunningham guesses that the gag is called a *mus* (mouse) because of *musis* (shut).

Hydra: monster that regrew two heads for every one cut off.

Klio: the Muse of history.

coat your tongue with honey: the sense would seem to be "sweeten your mouth, you're talking foul" and be the equivalent, with what a difference, of washing one's mouth with soap.

IV. WOMEN AT THE TEMPLE

The setting is a temple to Asklepios, god of healing, Kos. The time (calculable from the artists mentioned) is between 280 and 265 BC. A satire on bourgeois pretension to the appreciation of art. All the remarks, I would conjecture, are fashionable clichés of the time.

Paiêon: Asklepios. This prayer would be formulaic.
the snake: the animal form in which Asklepios appeared. One was kept in the temple, and frequently in houses.

V. THE JEALOUS WOMAN

The setting is a house of a well-to-do woman.

Davos: stock name for a butler in New Comedy.
Gerenia: nothing is known of this religious festival.

VI. A PRIVATE TALK BETWEEN FRIENDS

The setting as a private house.

dildo: the Greek is *baubon*, a leather penis for masturbation. The word means "a pacifier." Sappho's word was *olisbos*. Herondas takes this household article for granted.

VII. THE SHOEMAKER

Cunningham and every editor and commentator of Herondas spend a lot of time explaining that this *mimiambos* is about women shopping for a *baubon*. This error arises from a similarity of stock comedy names. Despite the names Metro and Kerdon, this play is not a sequel to VI. For the life of me, all I see in this playlet is the perennial comedy of women looking at every pair of shoes in a shop and leaving without buying any: this is the original of Blondie at the shoestore.

cabinet: the word may be simply *shoebox.*
artist's beeswax: Greek painters mixed their colors in wax.
Mikion's wild beasts: a local zoo or menagerie?
Women and dogs eat shoes: Cunningham has a long note on shoe fetishism, which he tries to tie in with his conviction that the shoes are not shoes but dildoes, but the proverb seems transparent to me: dogs chew up shoes and women

wear them out and buy them with frantic regularity. Human nature is constant, and I assume that Greek women of the Alexandrian period owned, as women now, fifteen to every one pair of shoes belonging to their husbands.

VIII. THE DREAM

Most interpreters see this as a personal statement. It need not be. The papyrus is badly damaged, but the drift seems to be that a poet dreams that he is involved in a contest of balancing on greased wineskins, and that Dionysos and the ancient poet Hipponax are surrealistically in the dream. Herondas clearly took Hipponax as his master, wrote in his "limping" meter and archaic diction, and imitated his satiric stance before the world. If the statement is personal, it is a satiric self-portrait, and may have been written for a highly literate banquet audience rather than for a theatre or public performance.

Latmian: proverbial. Endymion sleeps forever in a cave on Mt. Latmos.

a short fawnskin tunic: this and the ivy crown identify the figure as the god Dionysos.

gift of Aiolos: a bag of wind. Wineskins, blown up and greased, were used as a game won by the contestant who could balance longest on one. The *some dived headfirst into the dust* four lines down describes people falling off wineskins.

Hipponax: Ephesian poet, sixth century BC, a bitter satirist.

r complete listing request free catalog from
w Directions, 80 Eighth Avenue, New York 10011   †Bilingual

For complete listing request free catalog from
New Directions, 80 Eighth Avenue, New York 10011

†Bilis